Happy St. Patrick's Day

Cute and Fun Coloring Book for Kids

KRISTINA CROSLOW

This Book
Belongs To:

Feeling
LUCKY

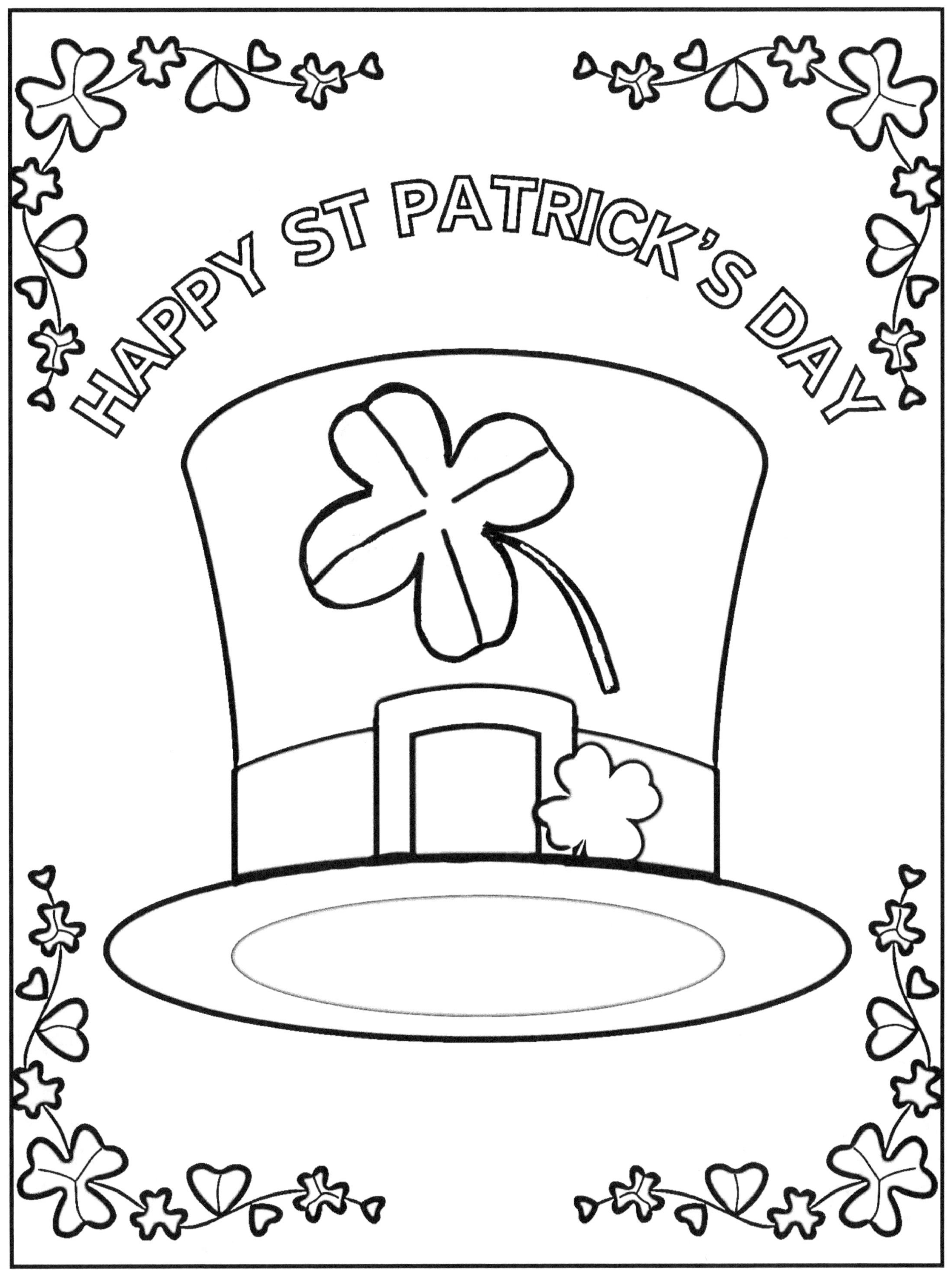

HAPPY ST PATRICK'S DAY

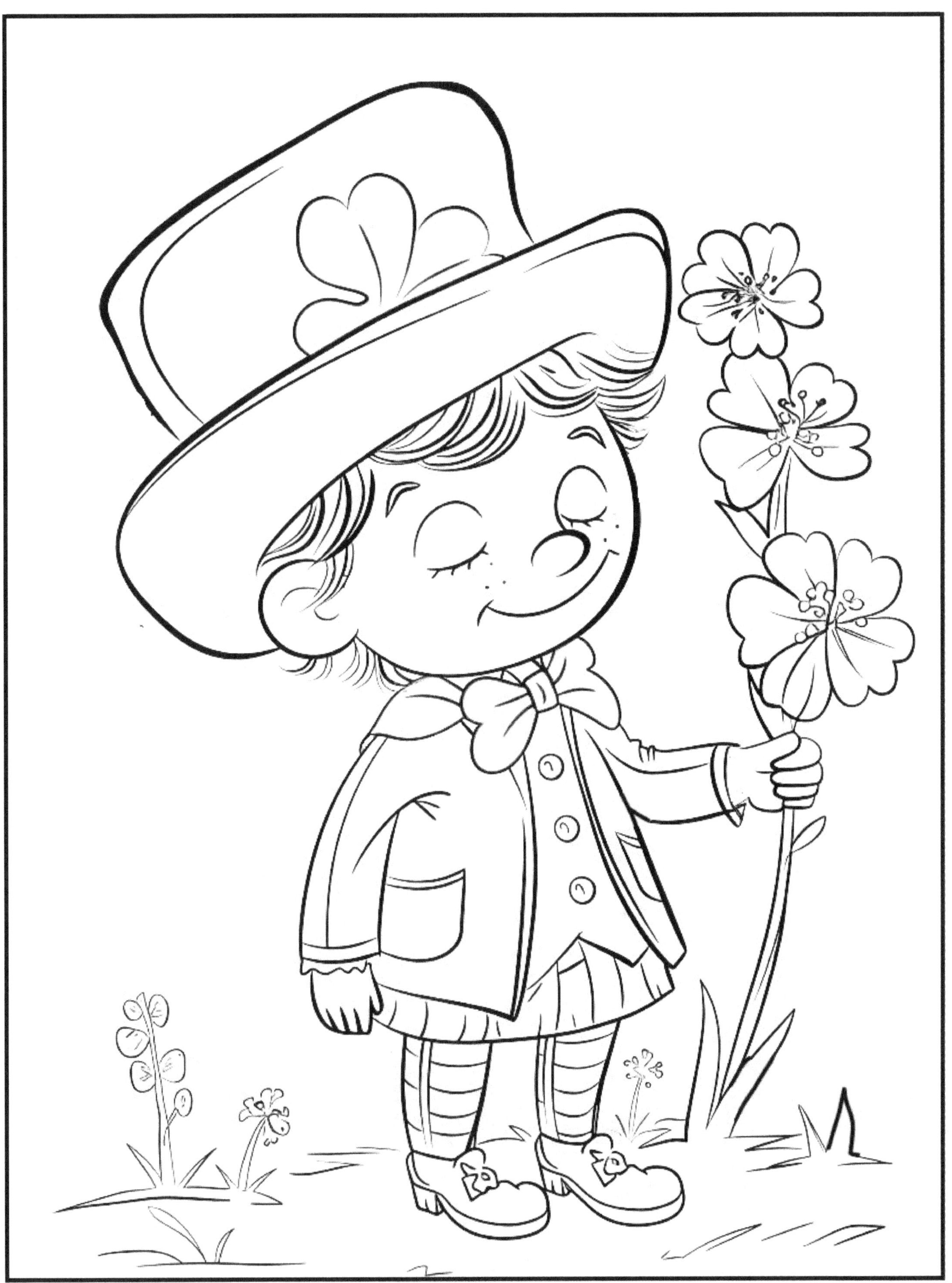

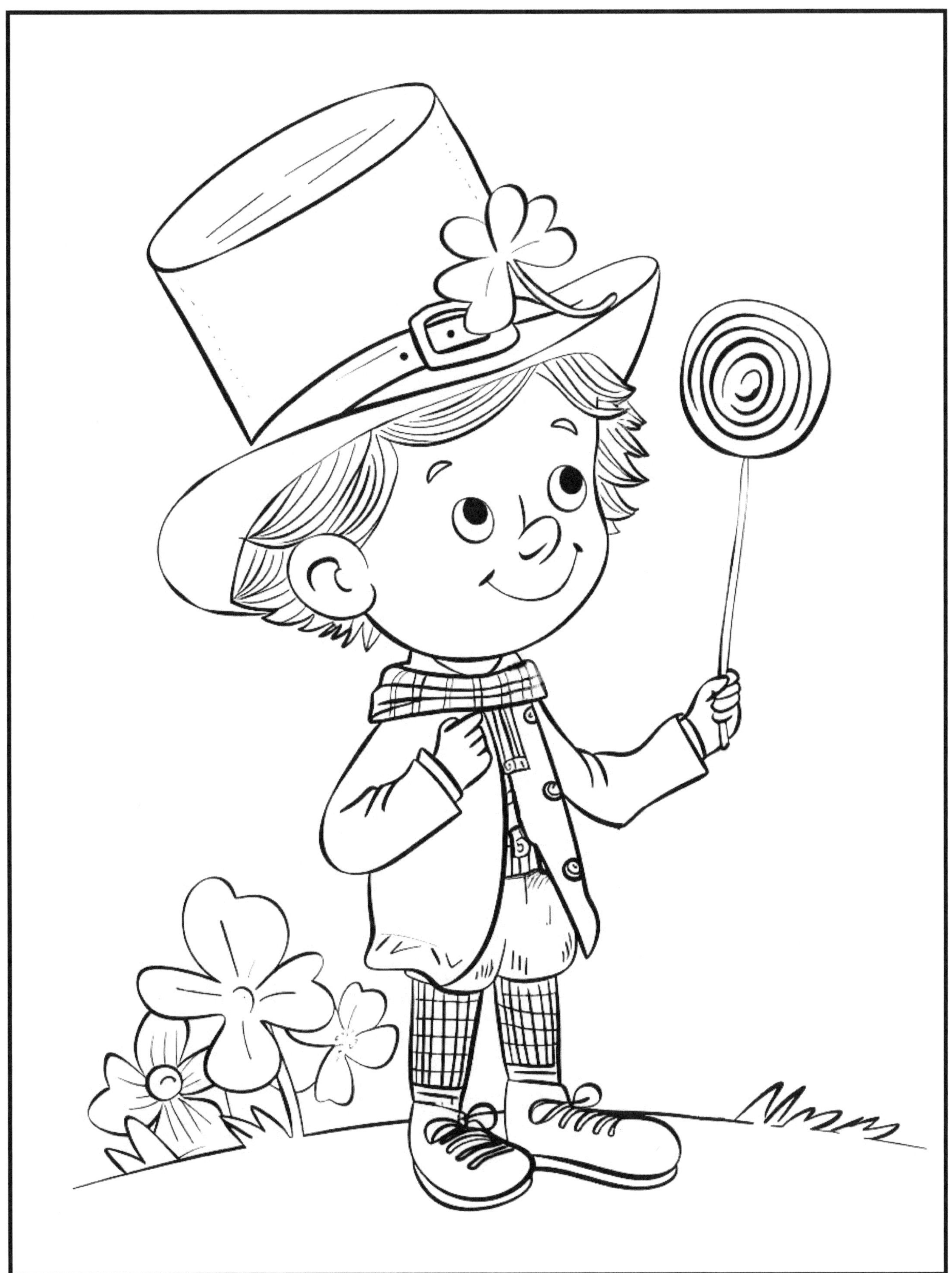

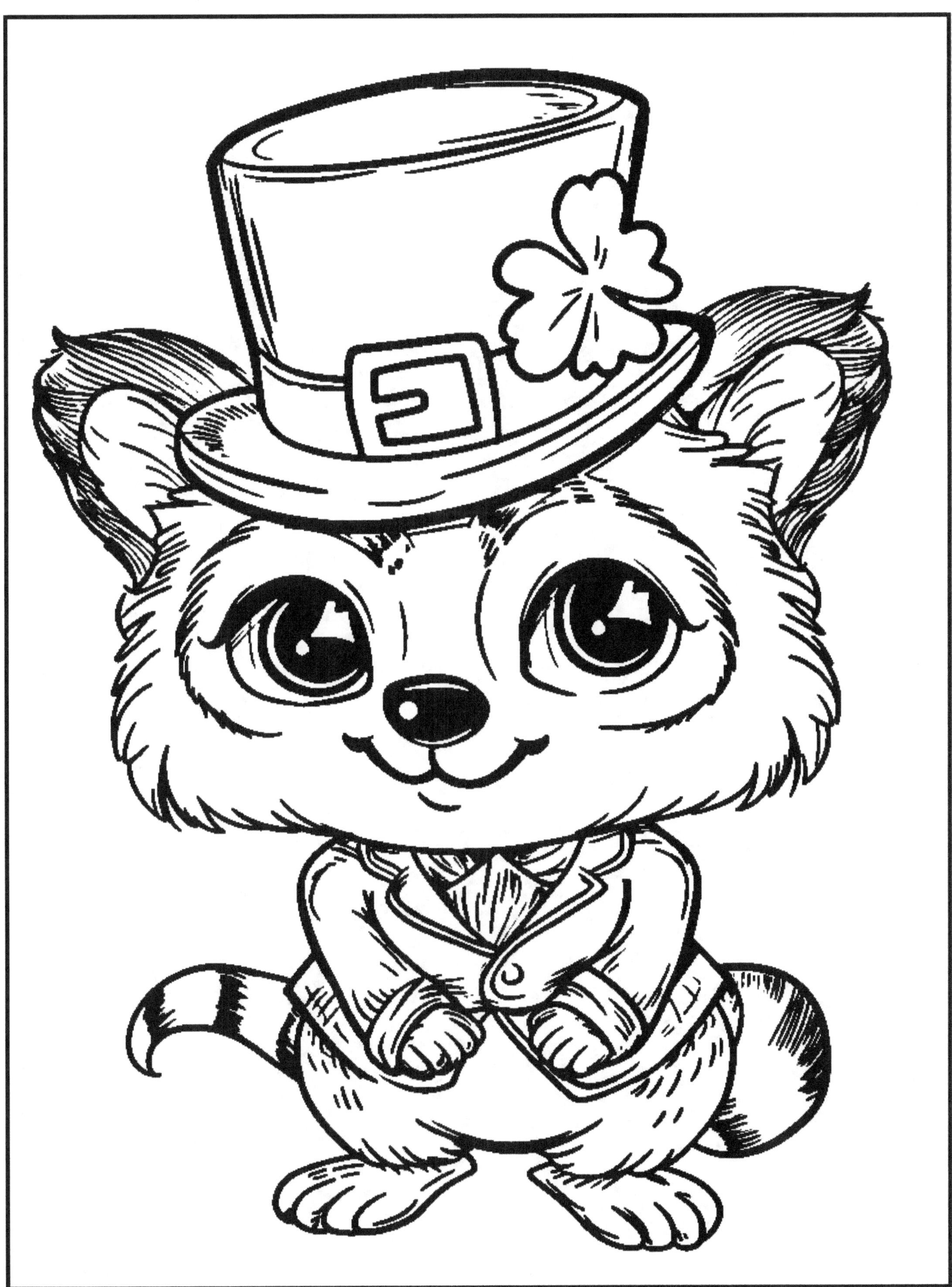

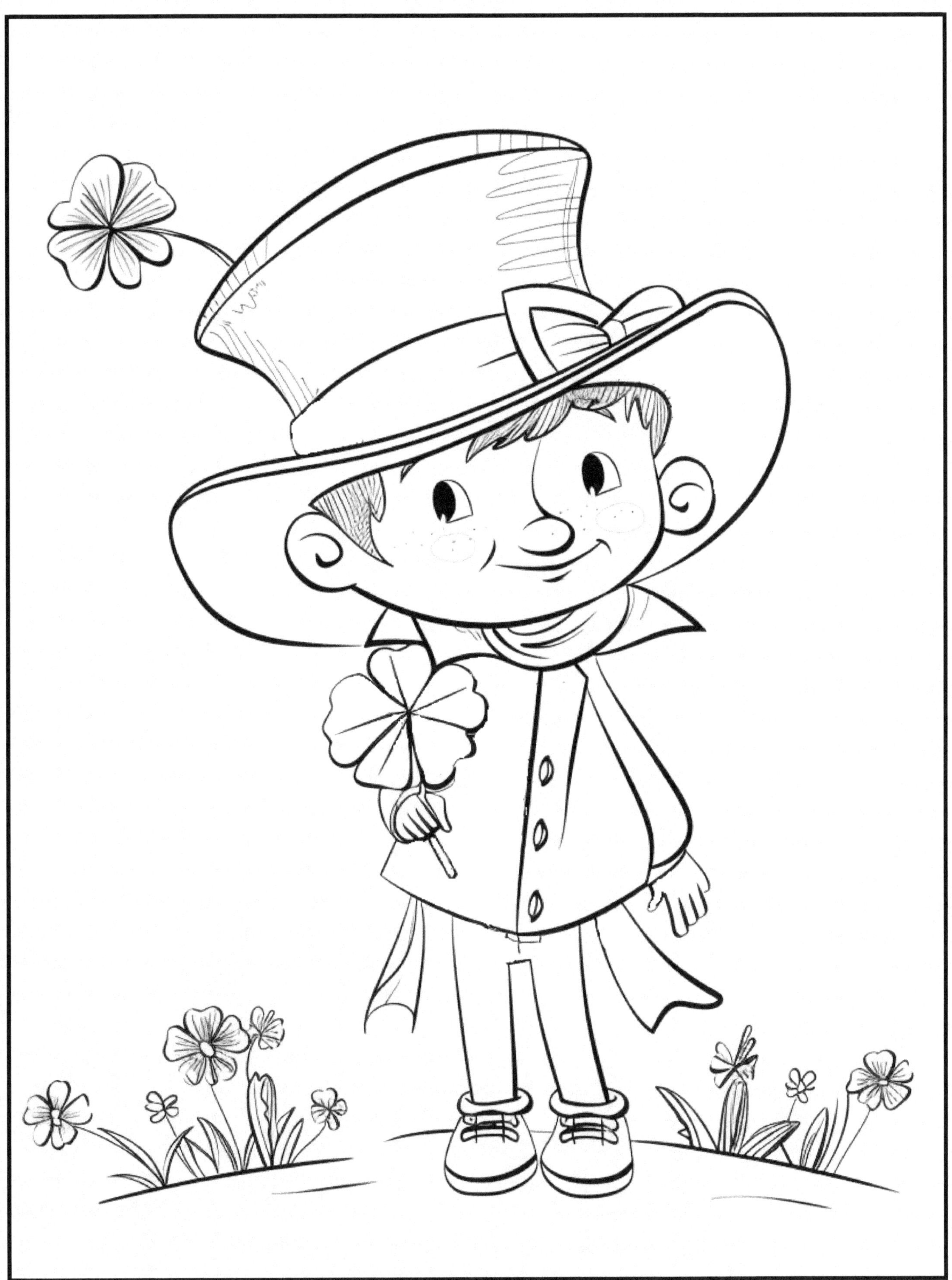

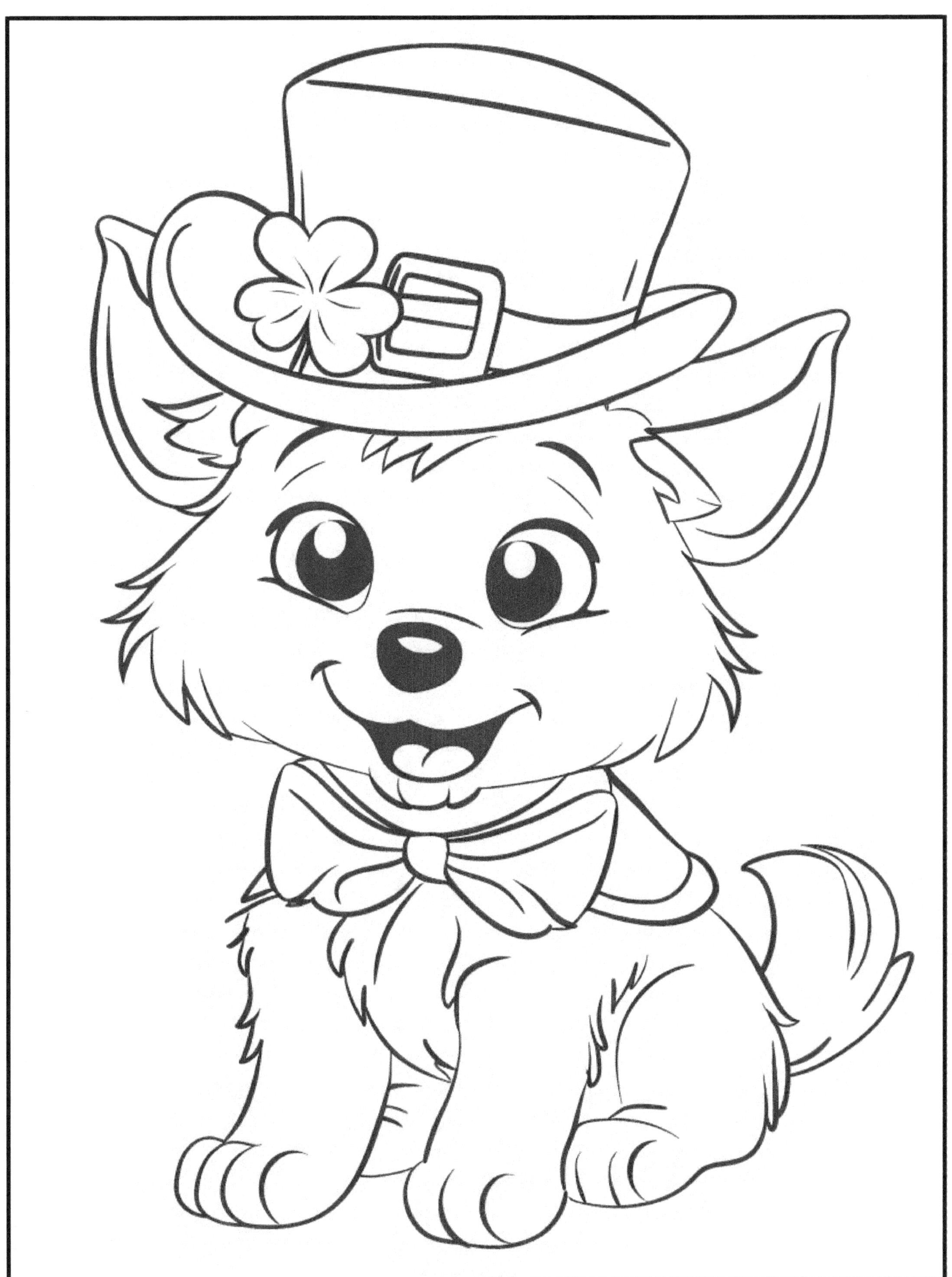

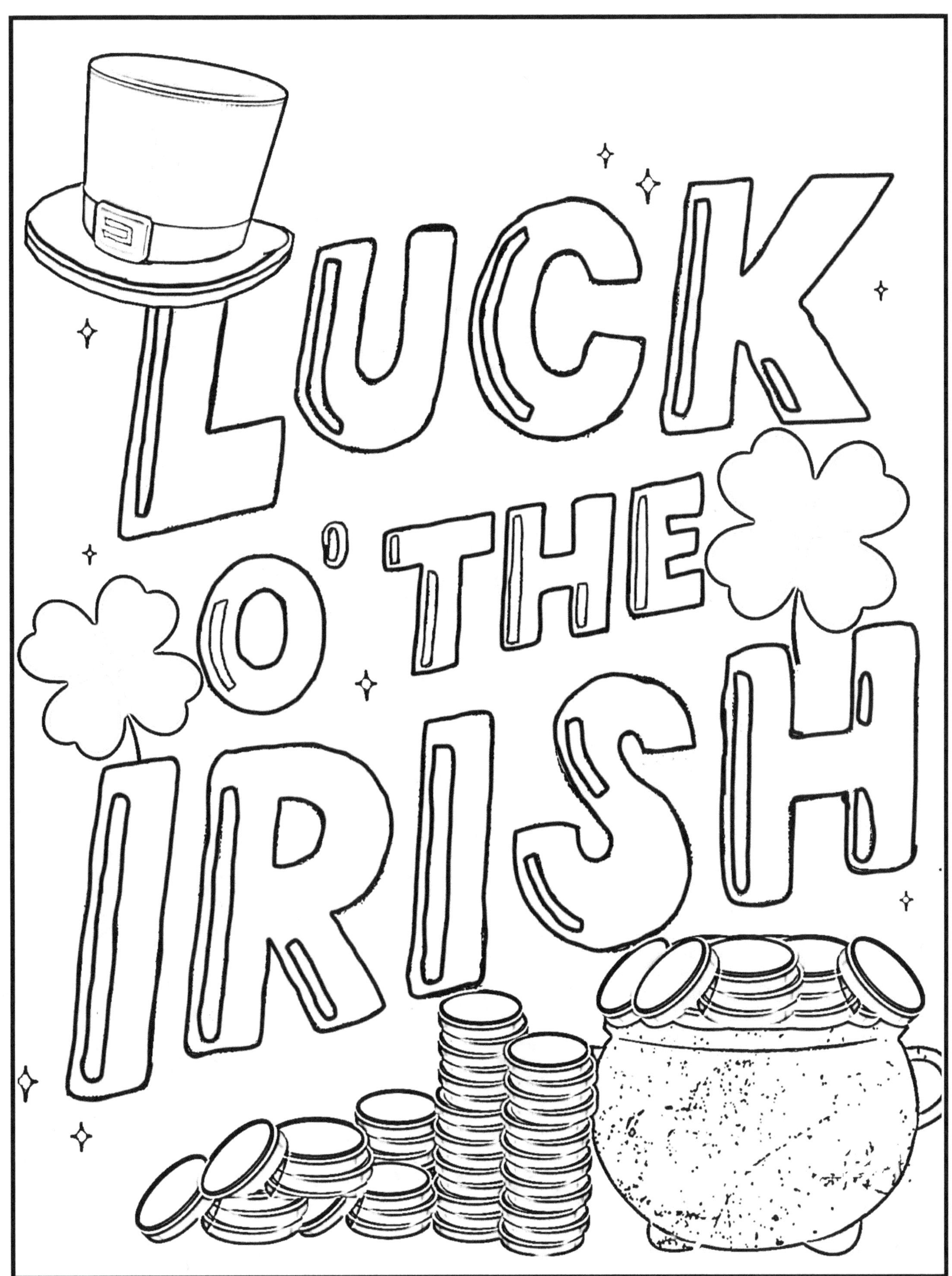

LUCK
O' THE
IRISH

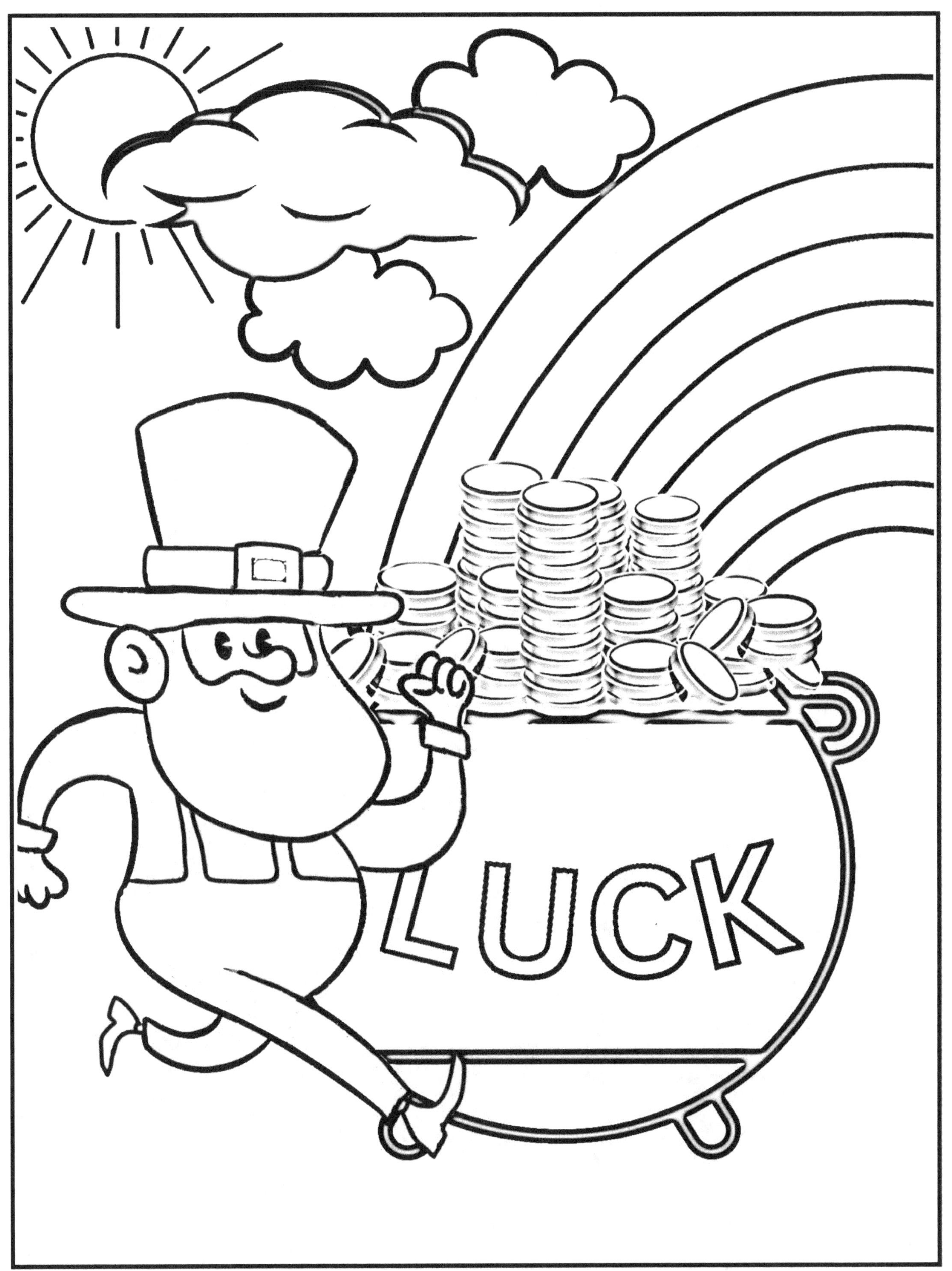
LUCK

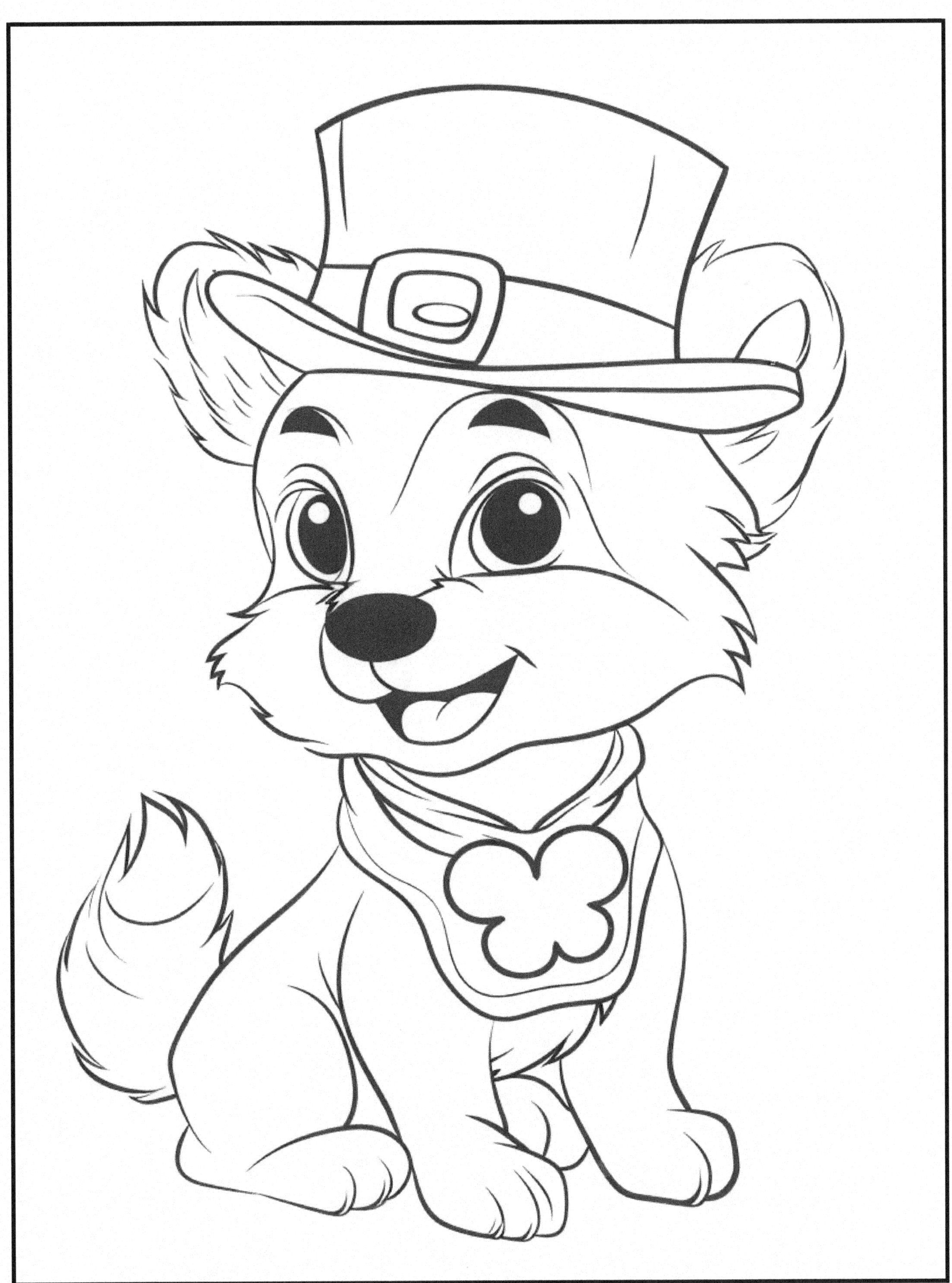

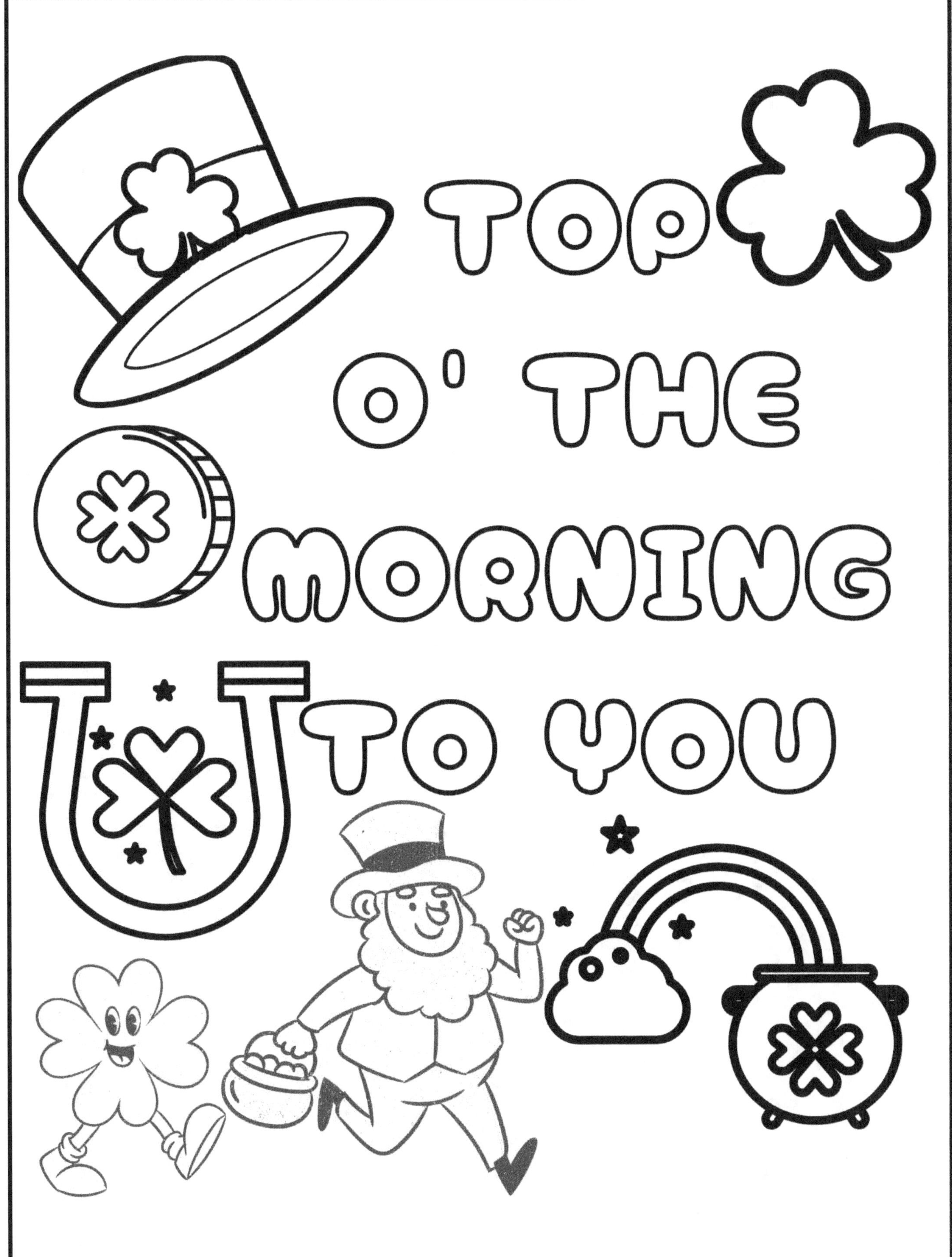

TOP
O' THE
MORNING
TO YOU

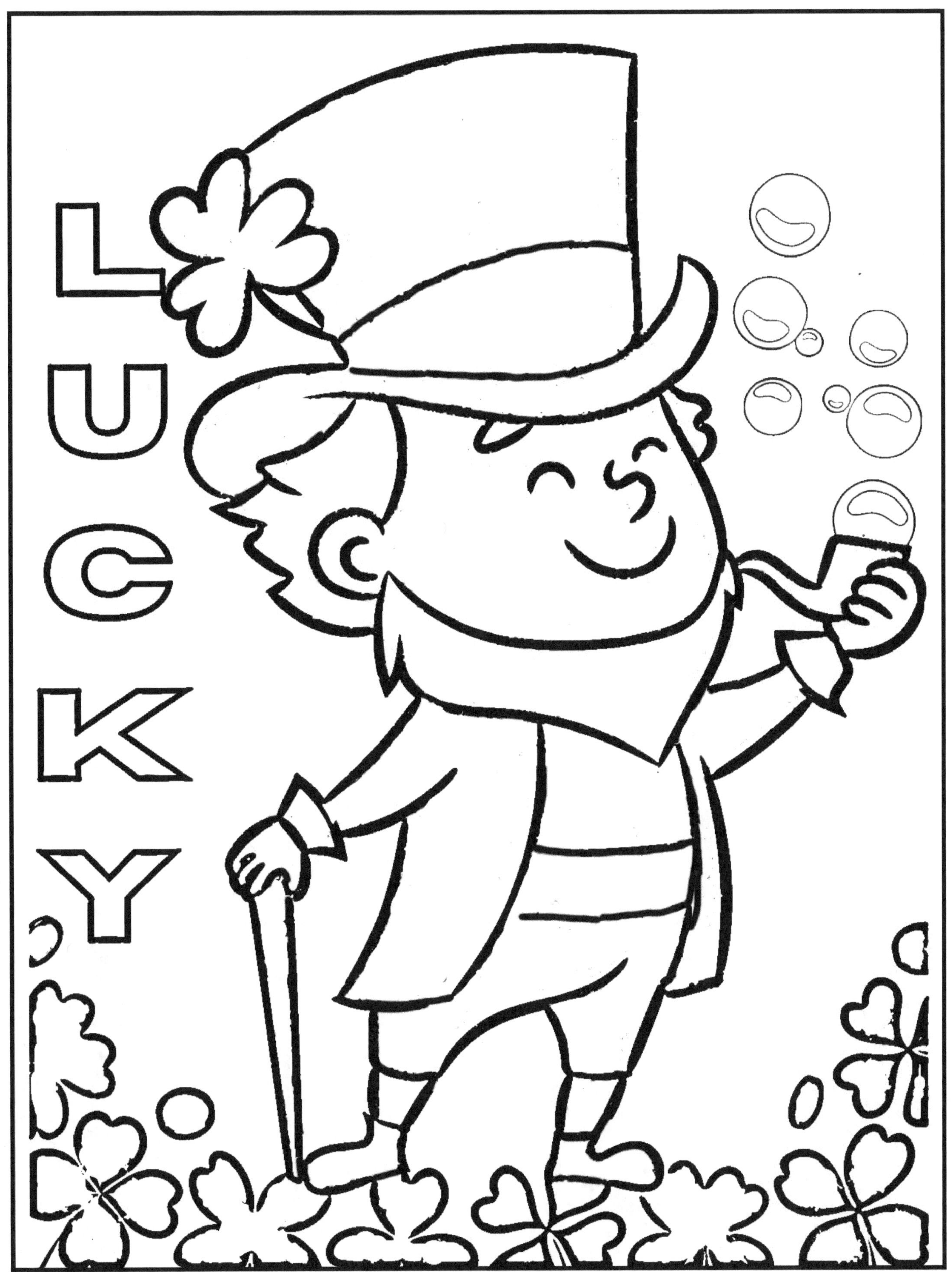

L
U
C
K
Y

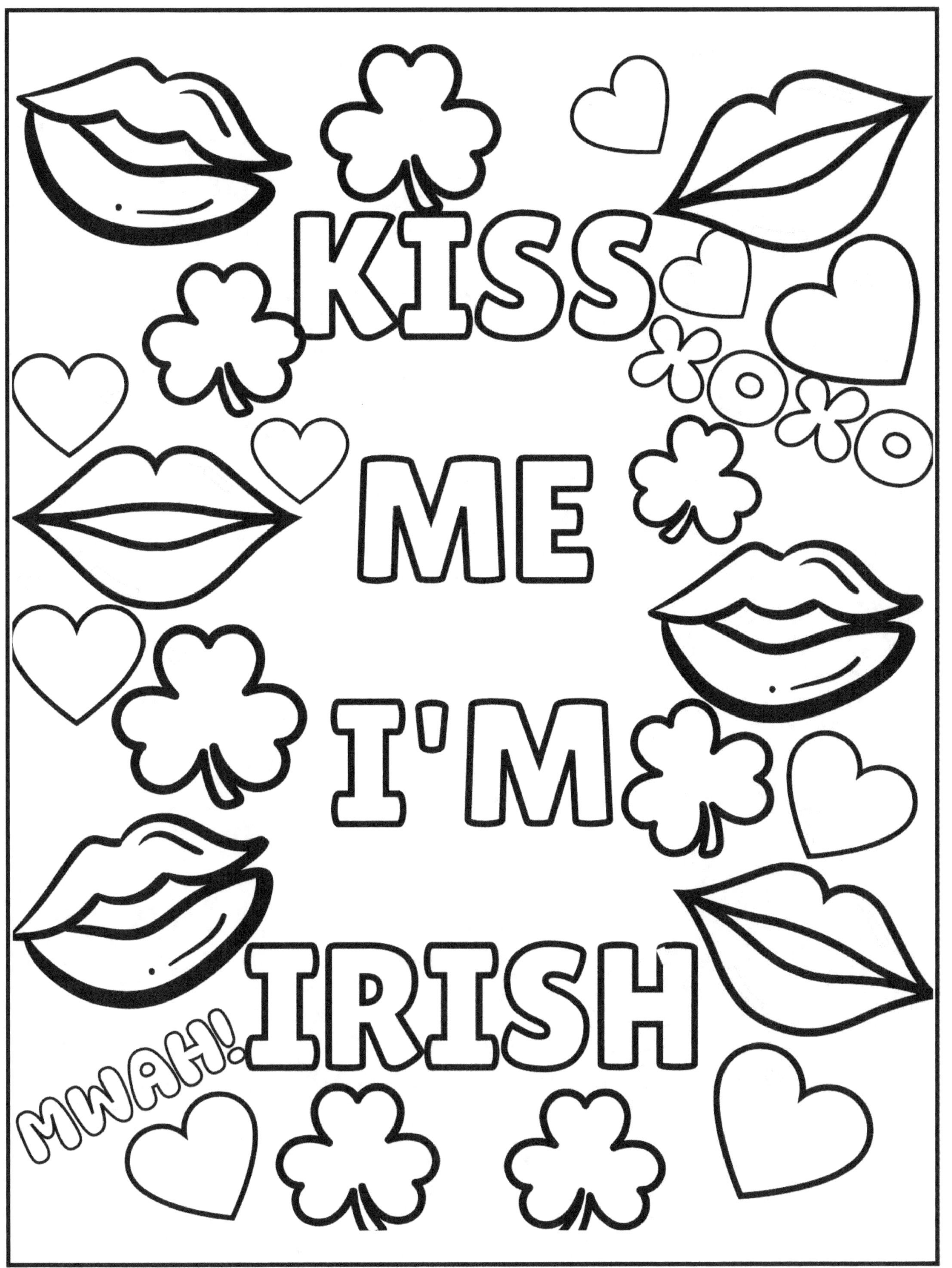
KISS
ME
I'M
IRISH
MWAH!

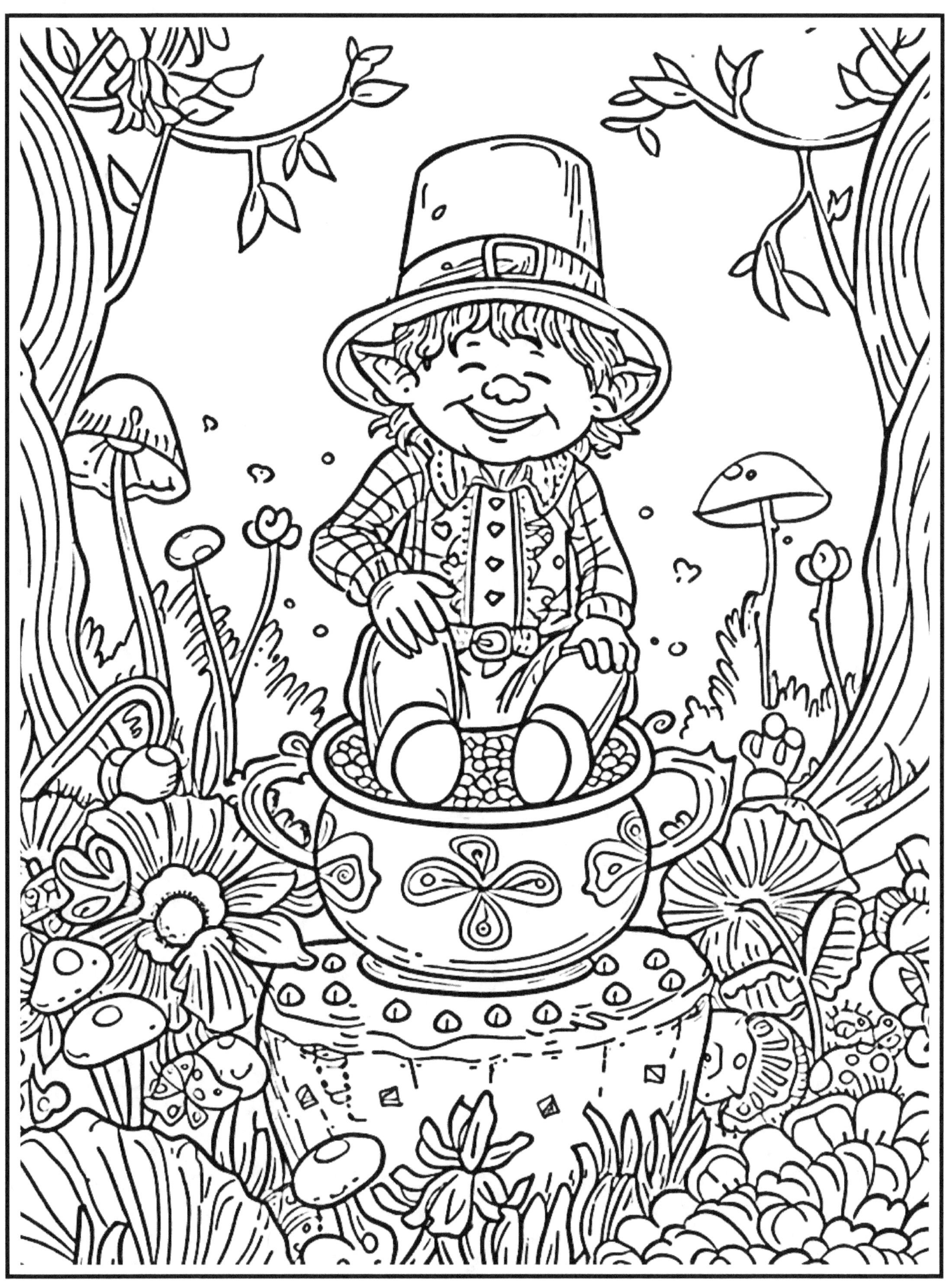

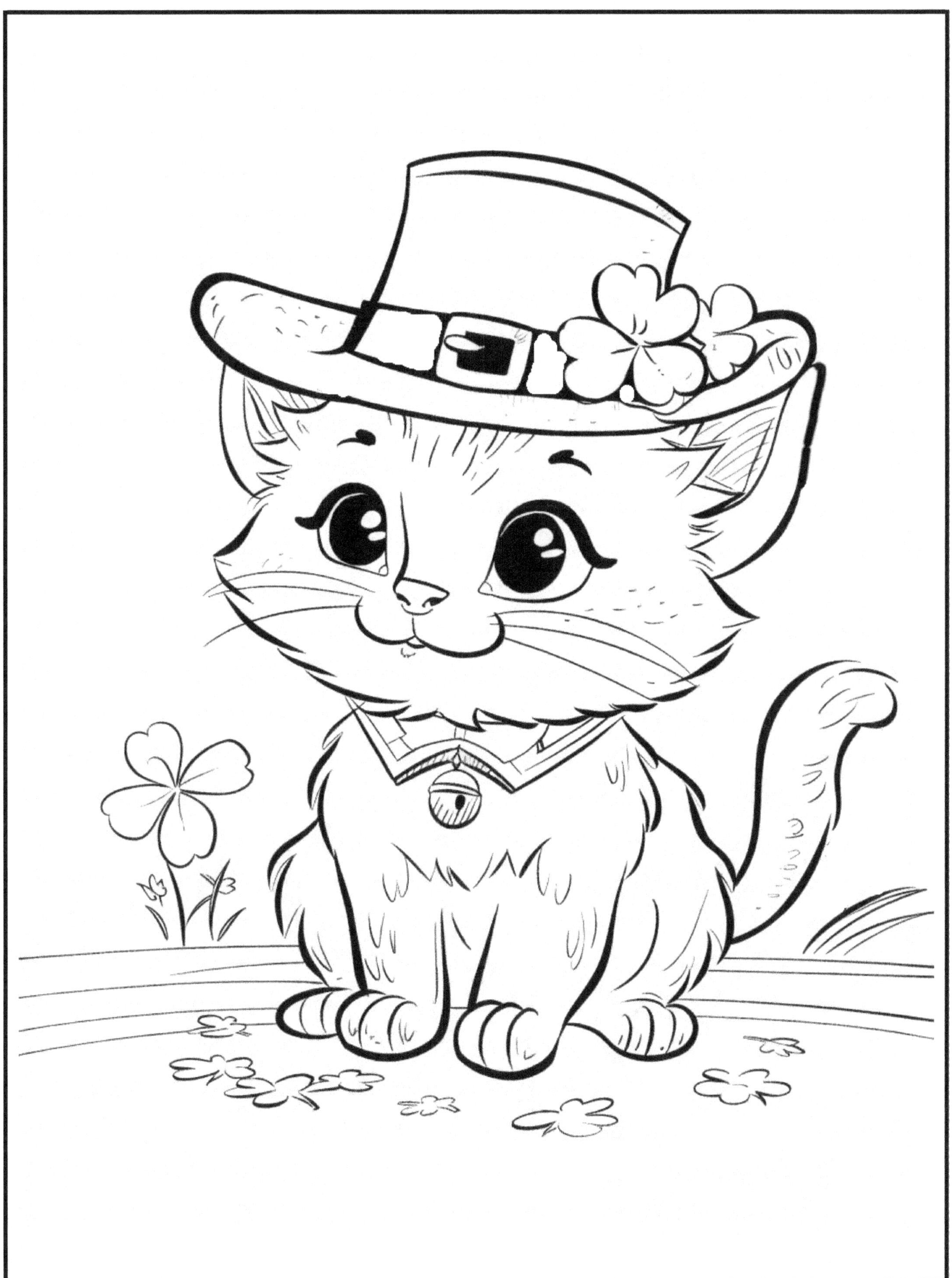

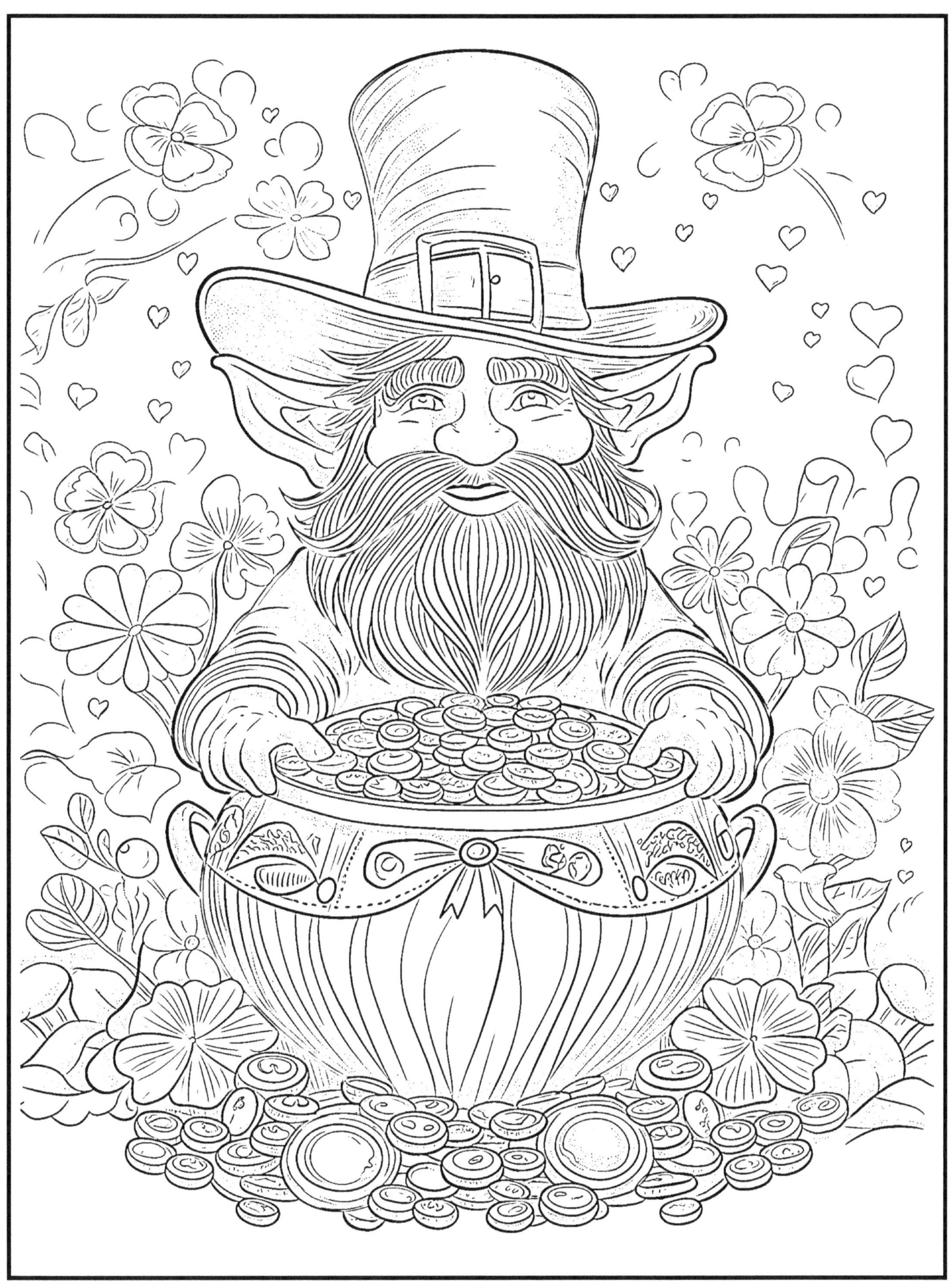

Draw your own Leprechaun to watch over the pot of gold!

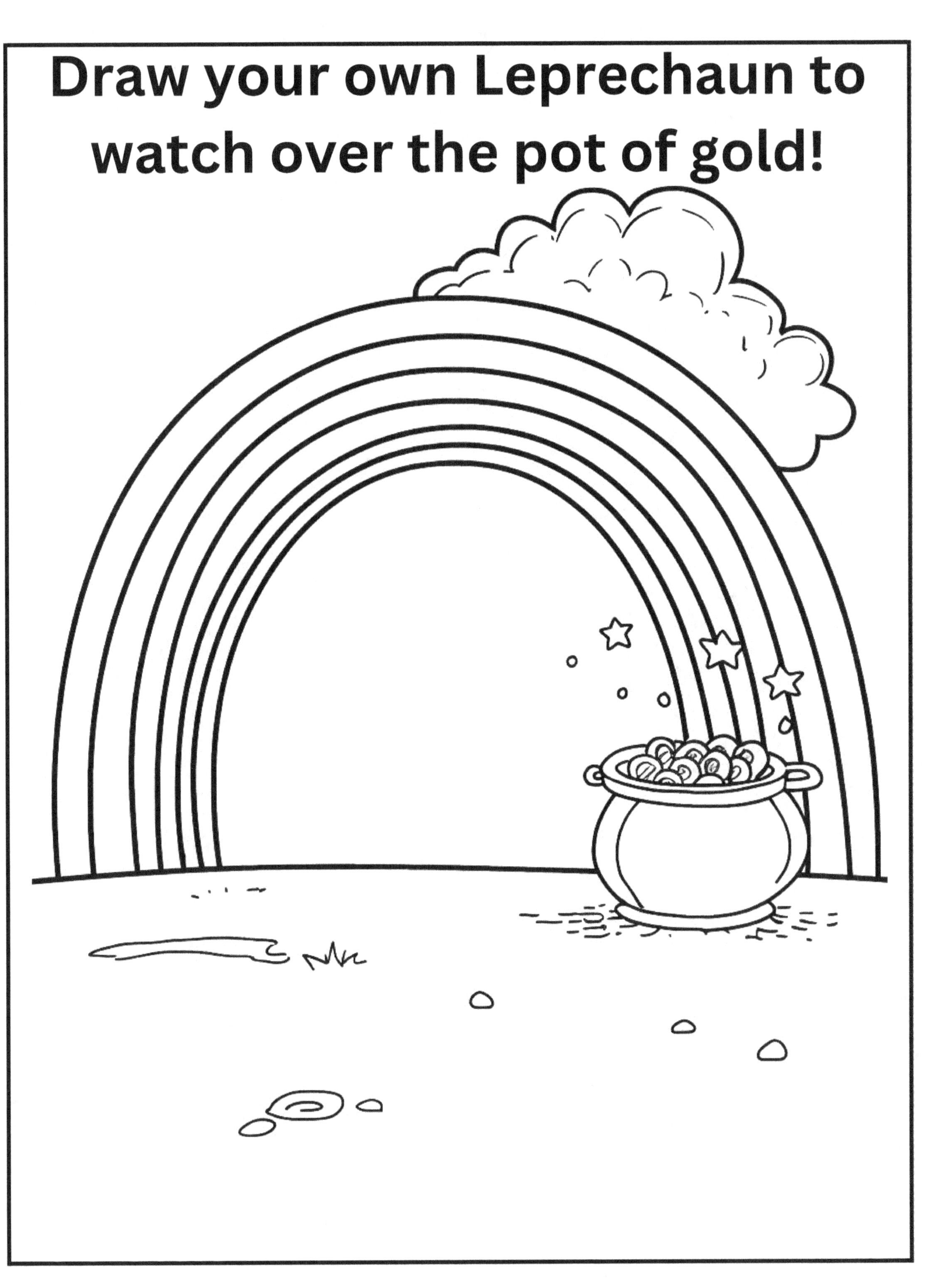

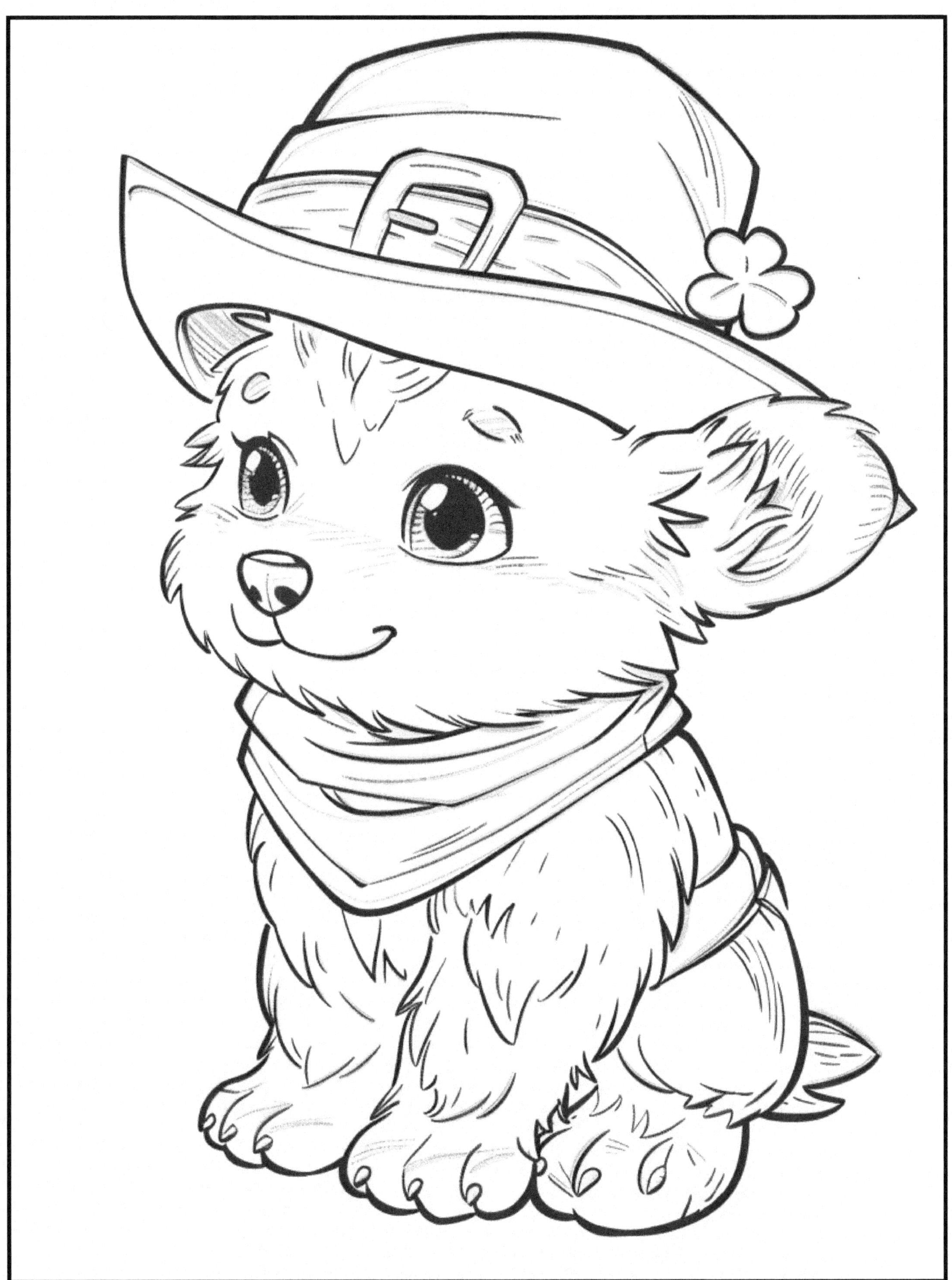

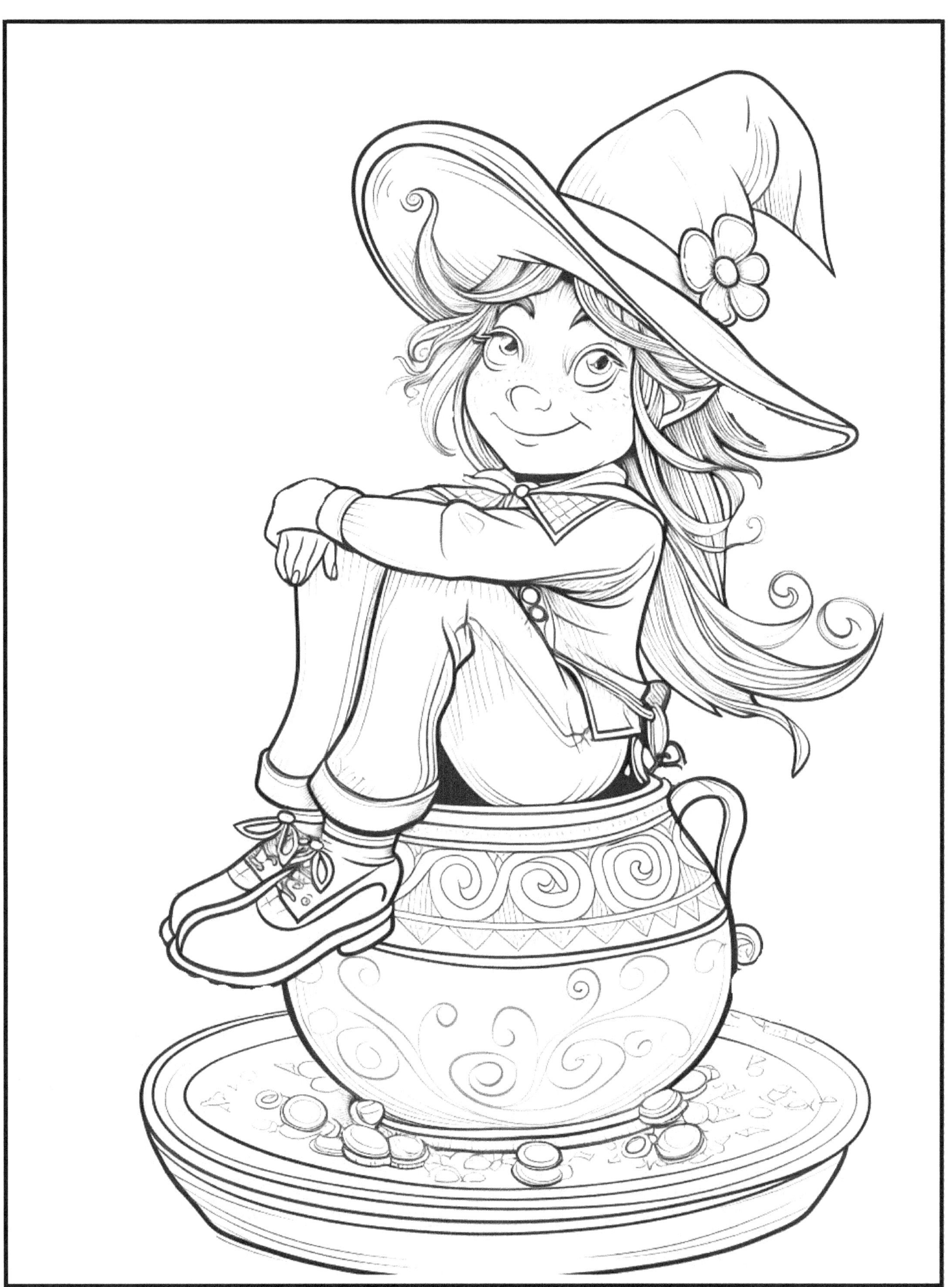

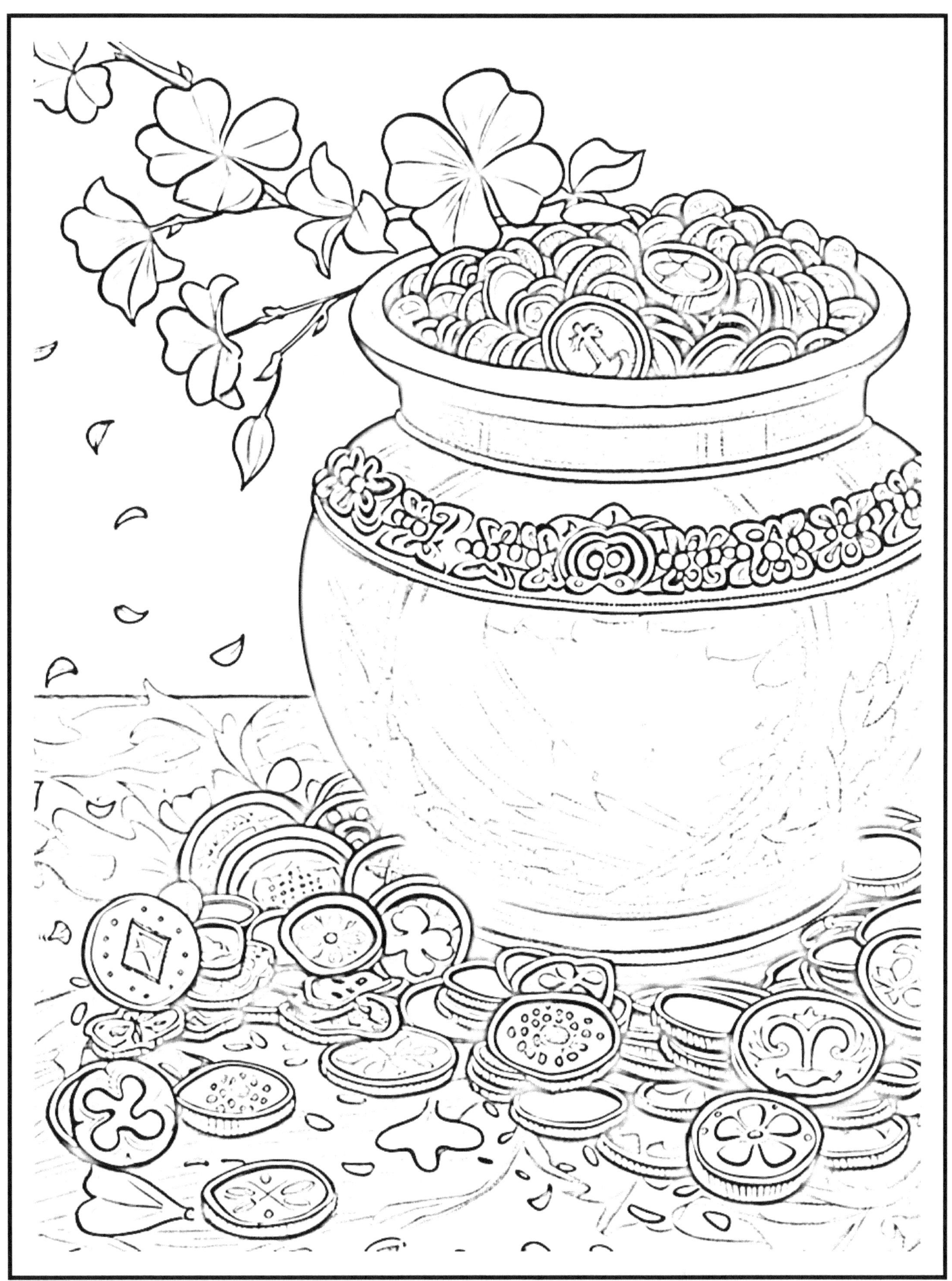

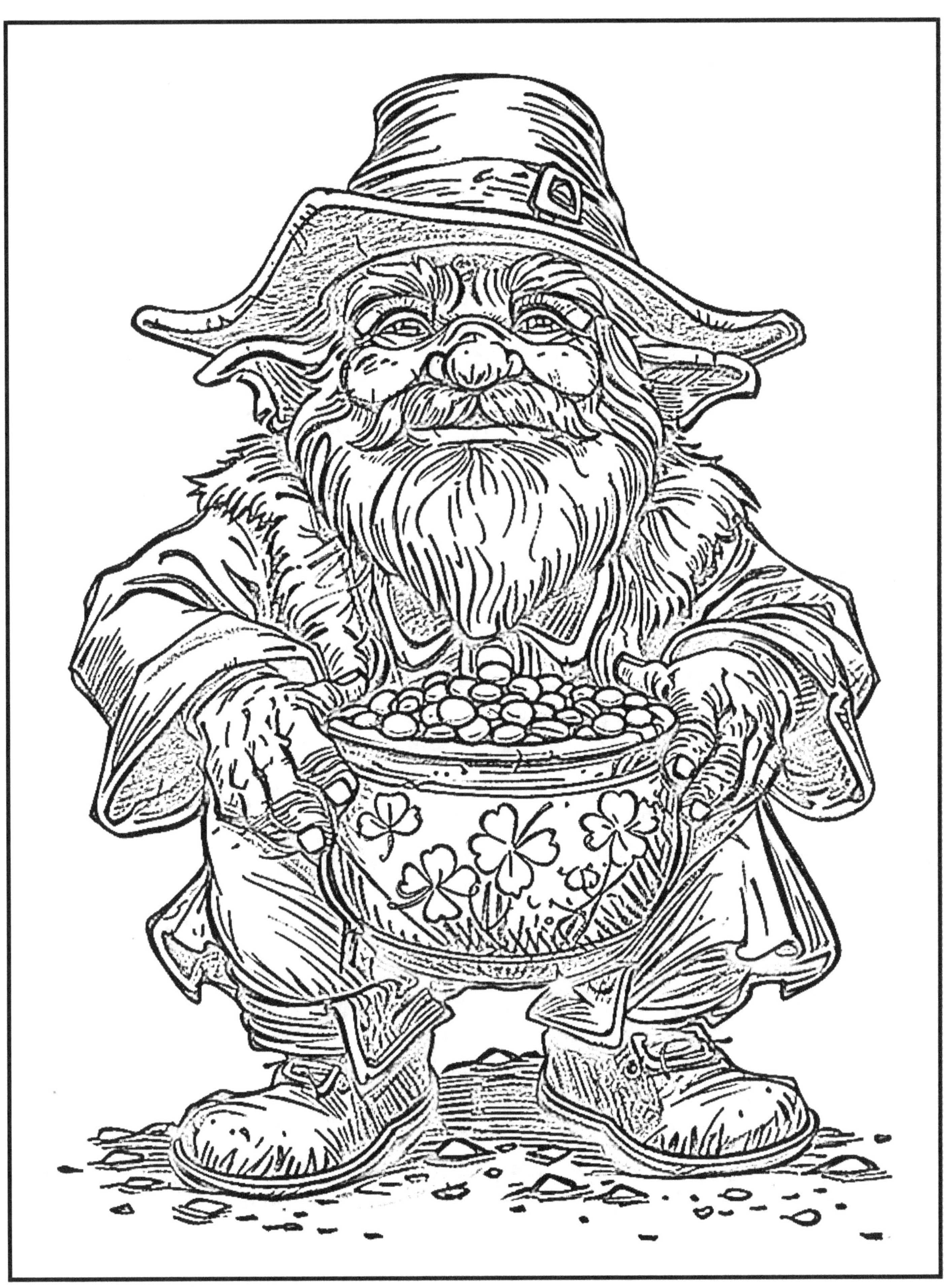

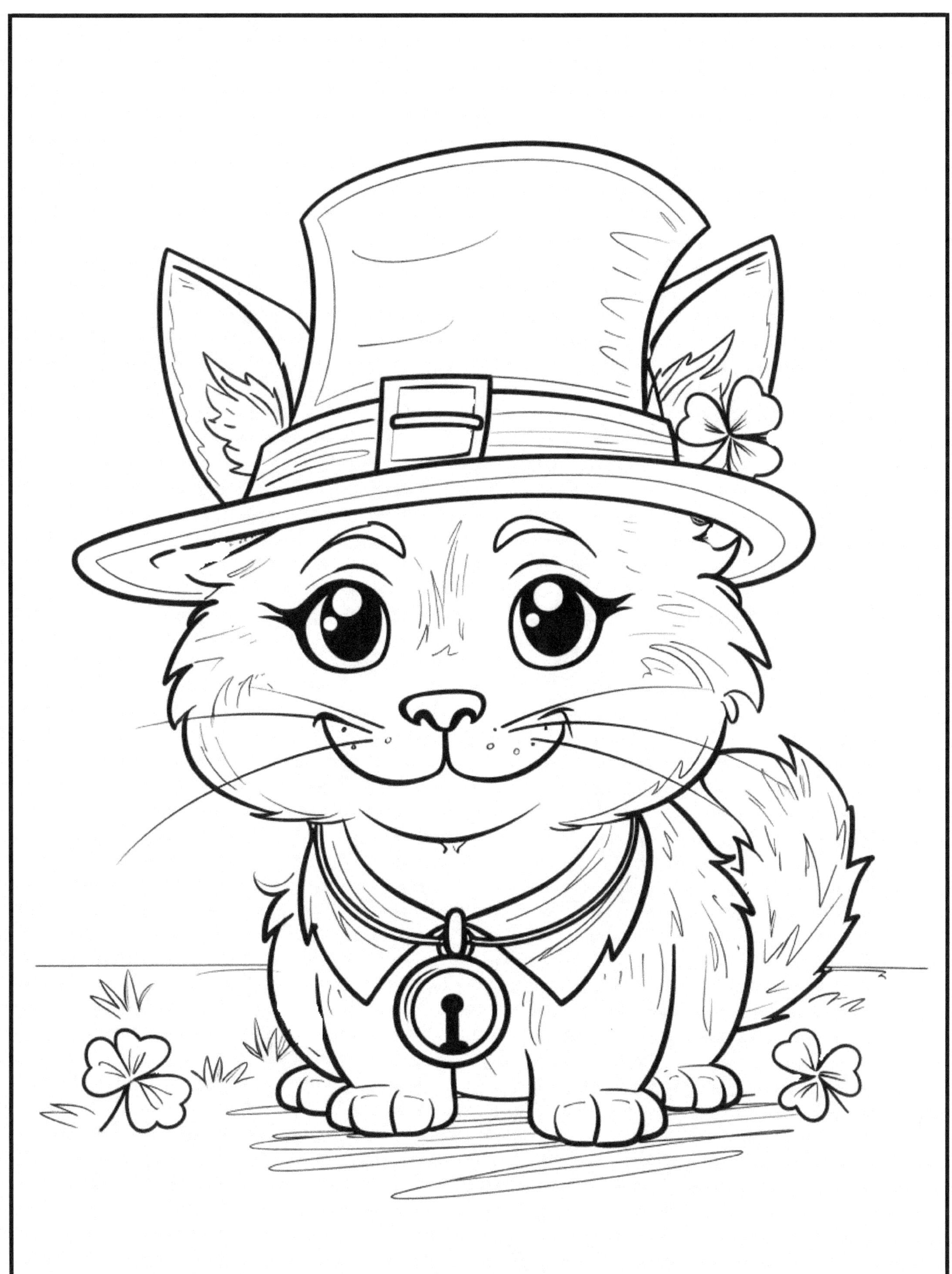

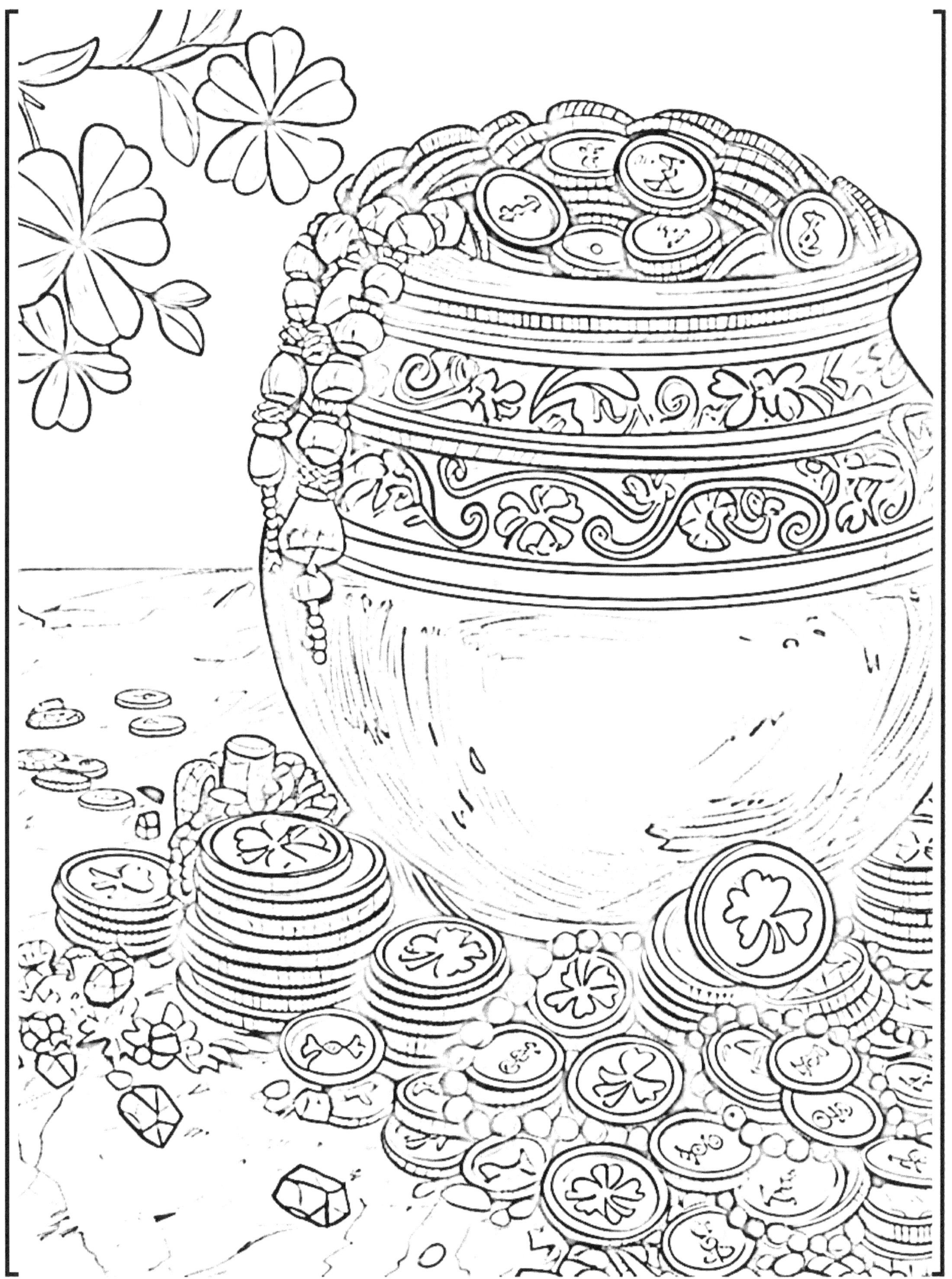

FEELING

LUCKY

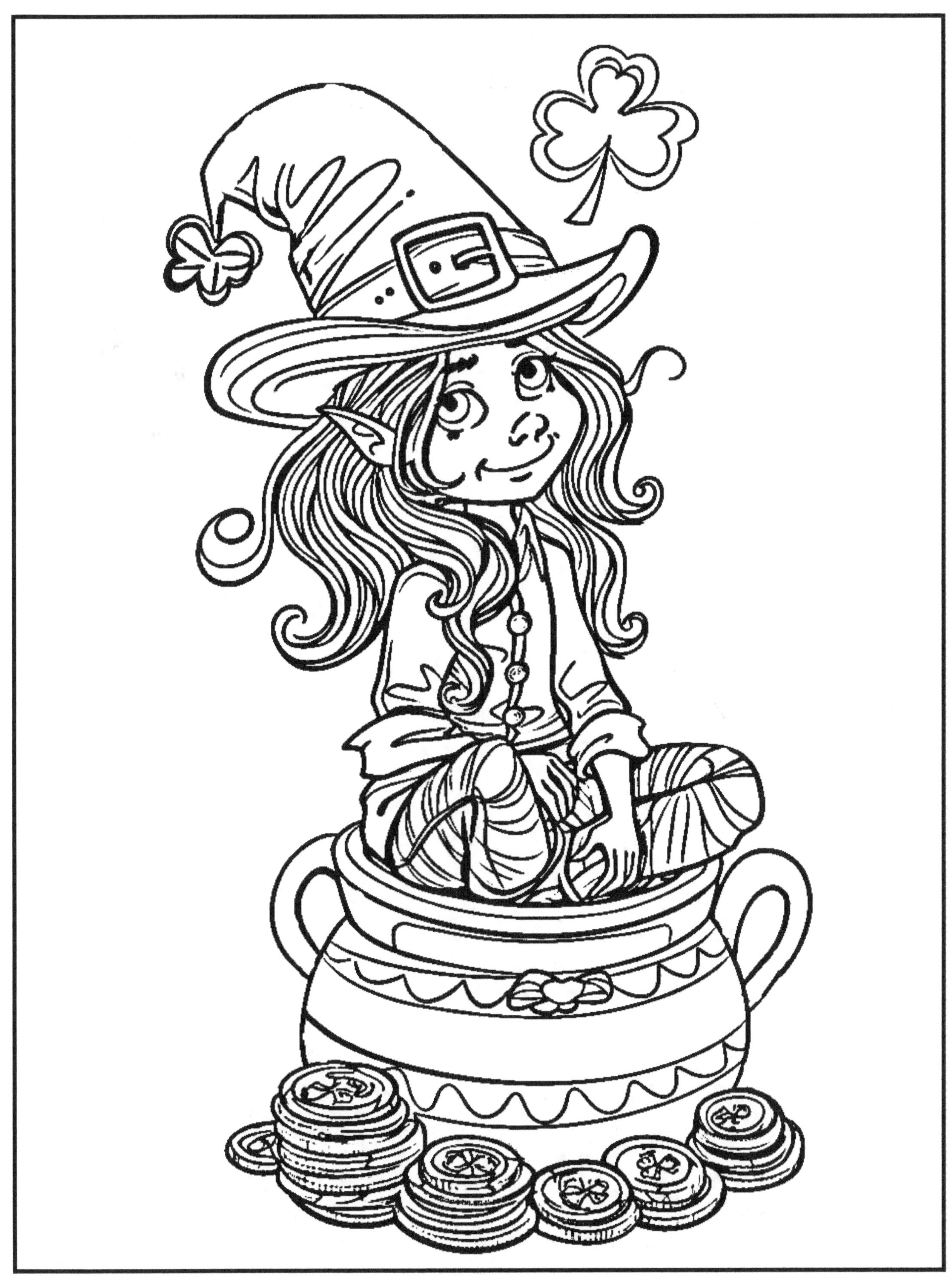

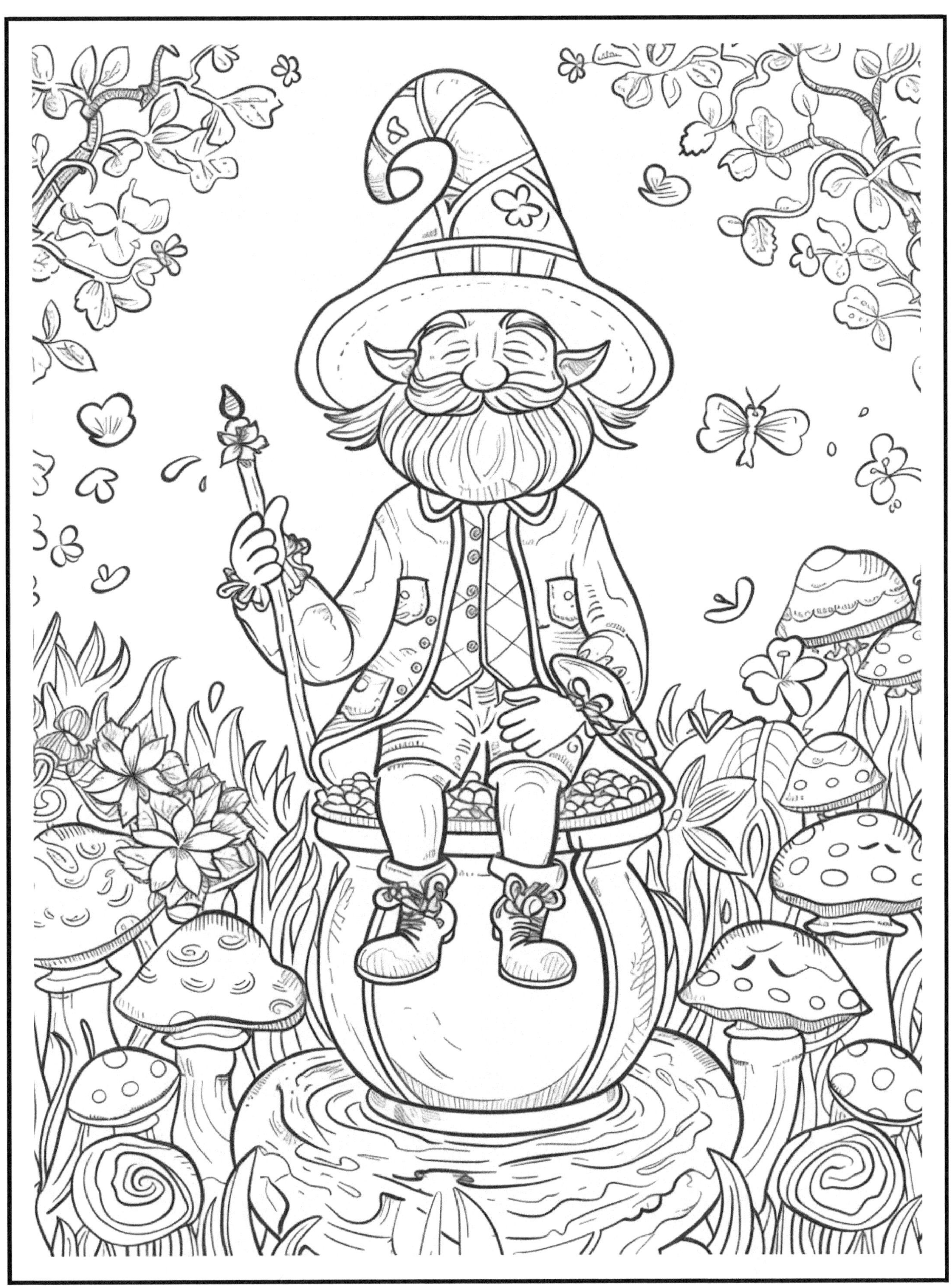

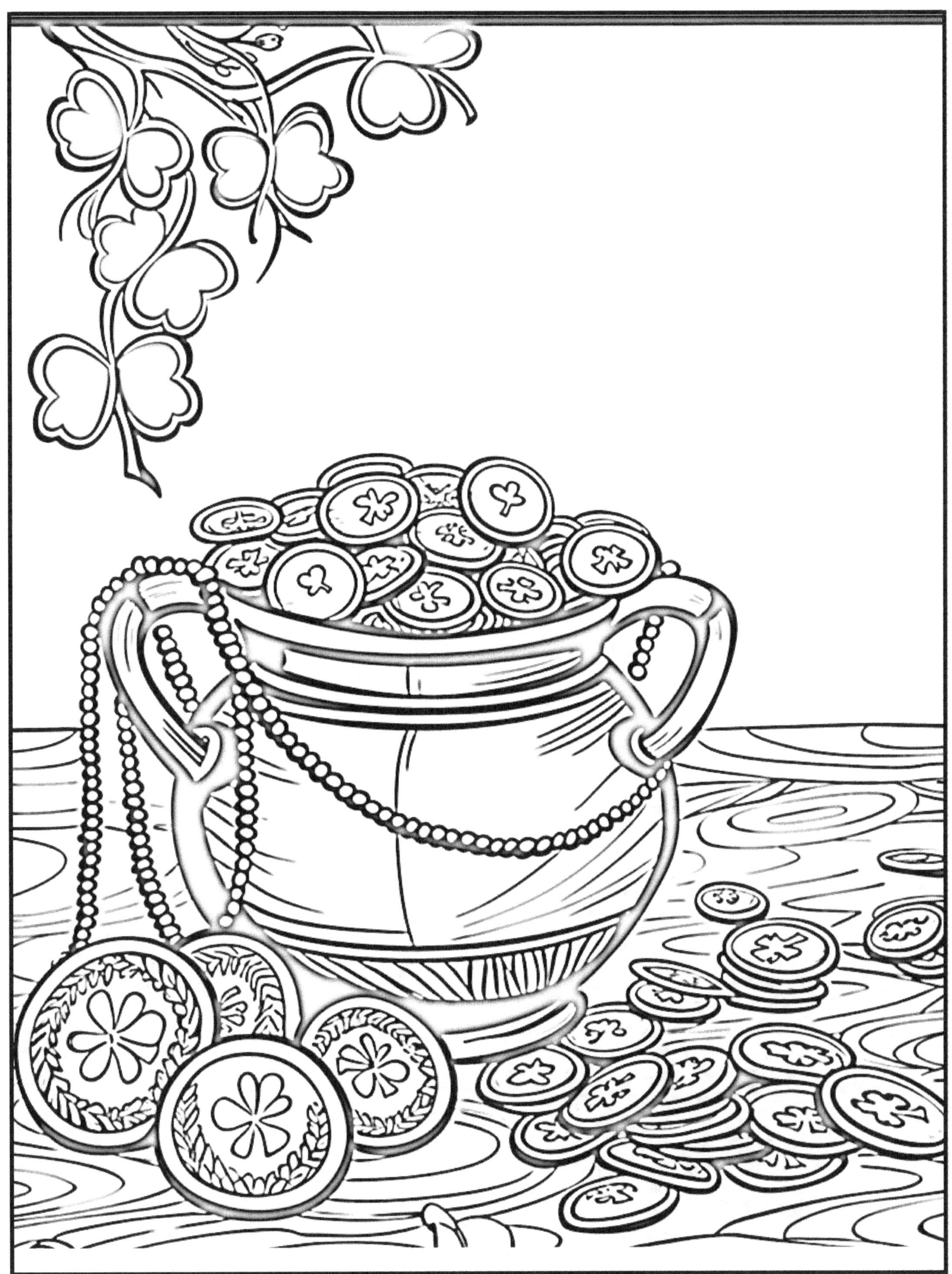

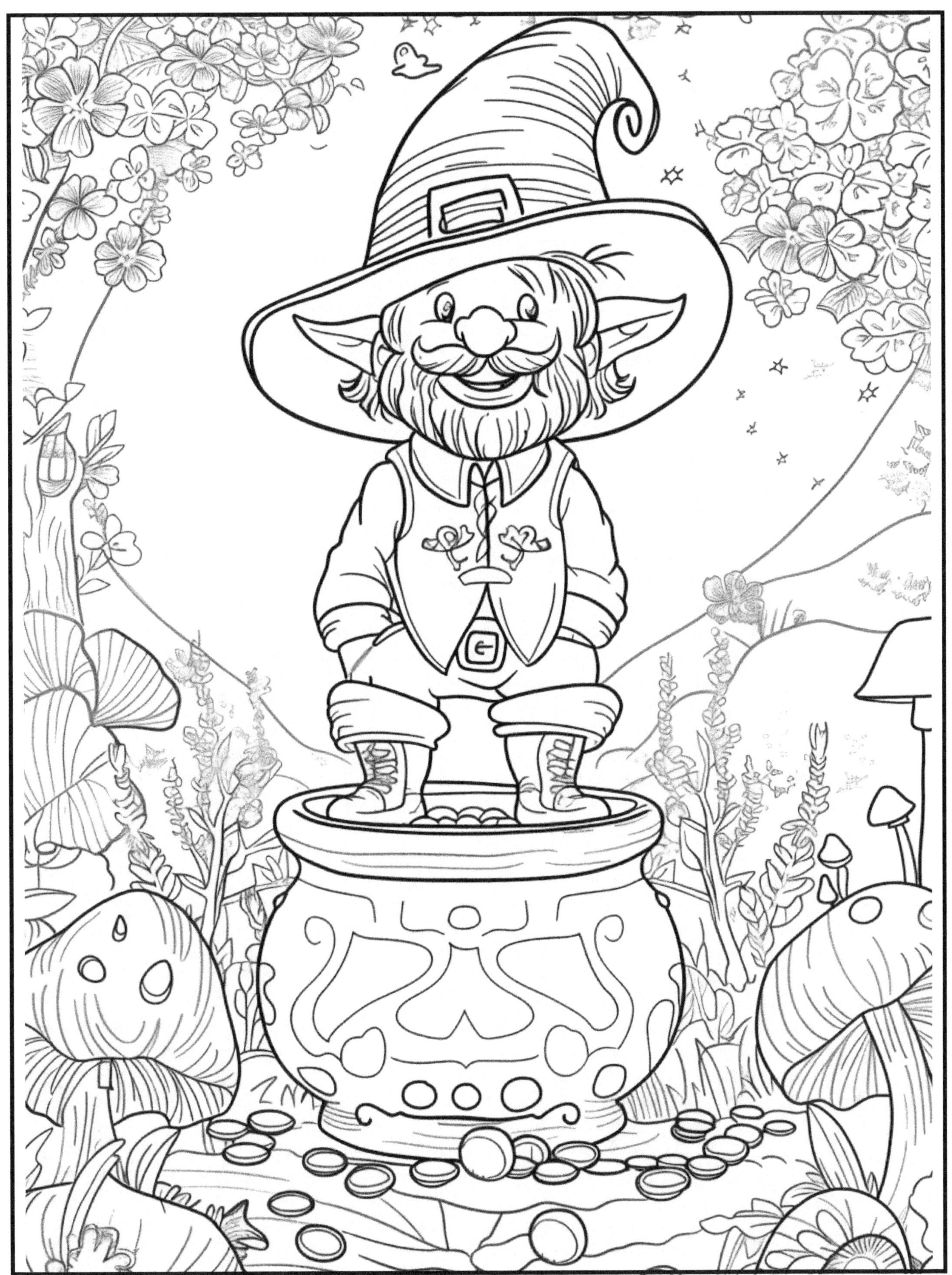

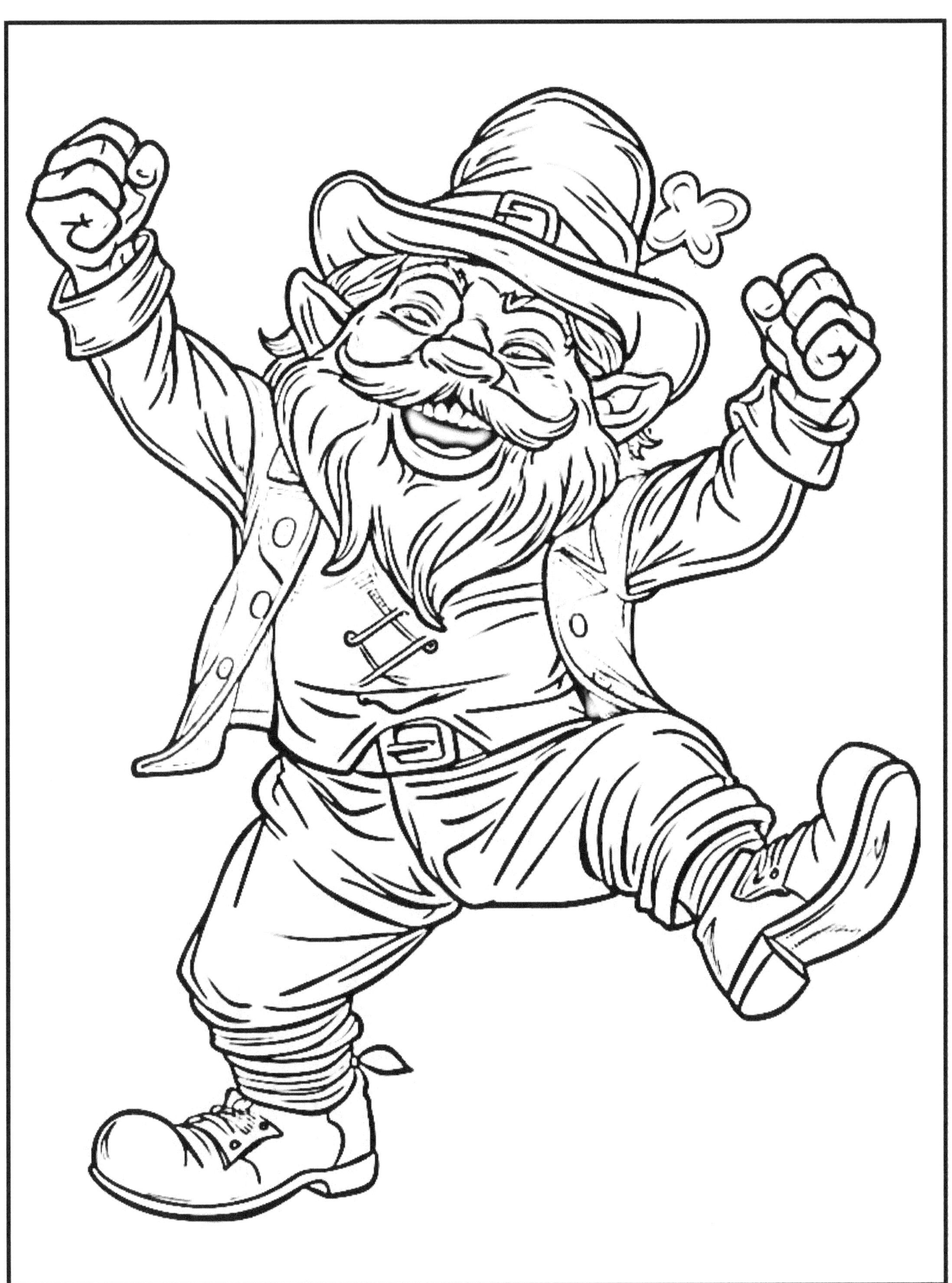

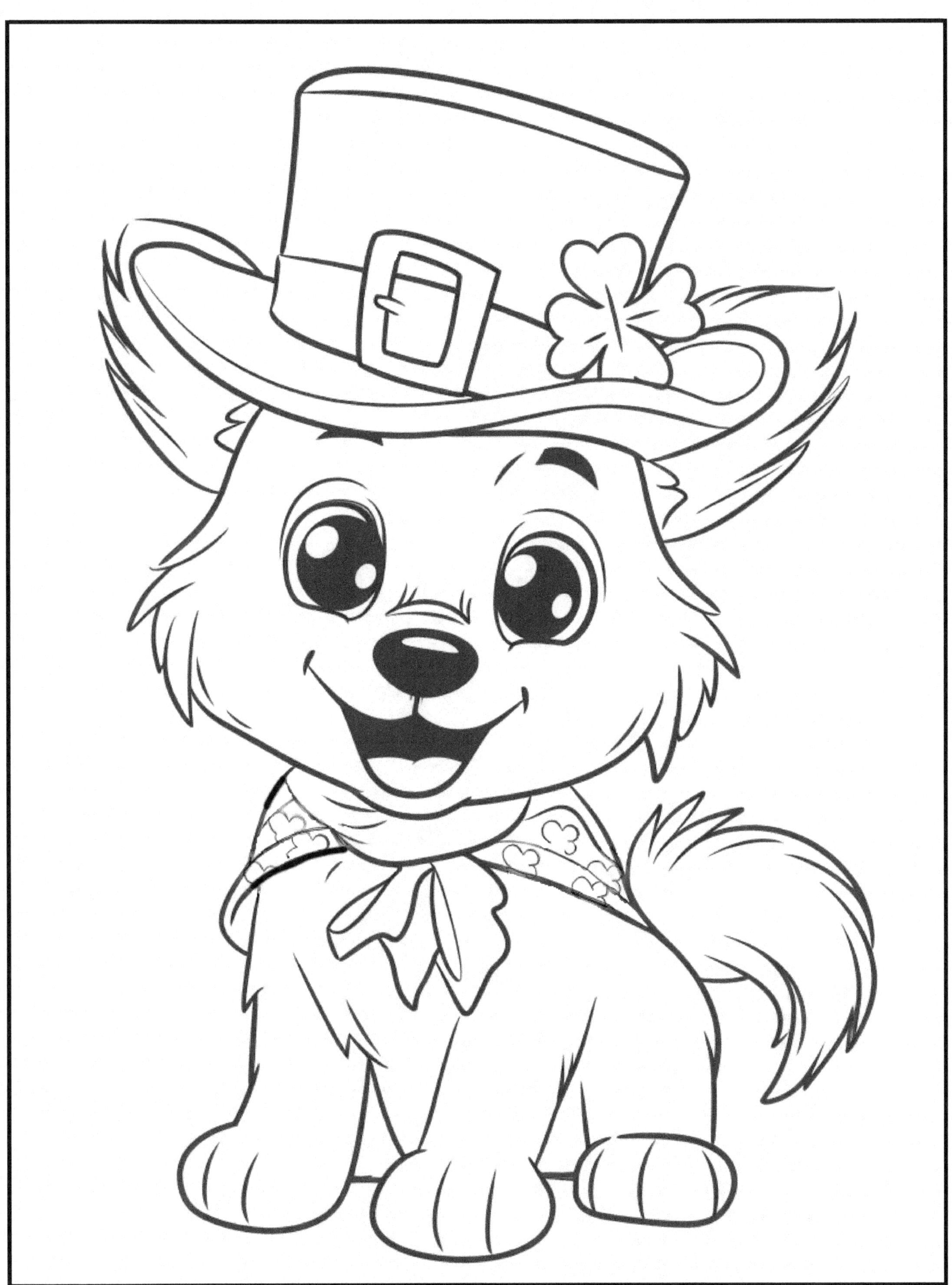

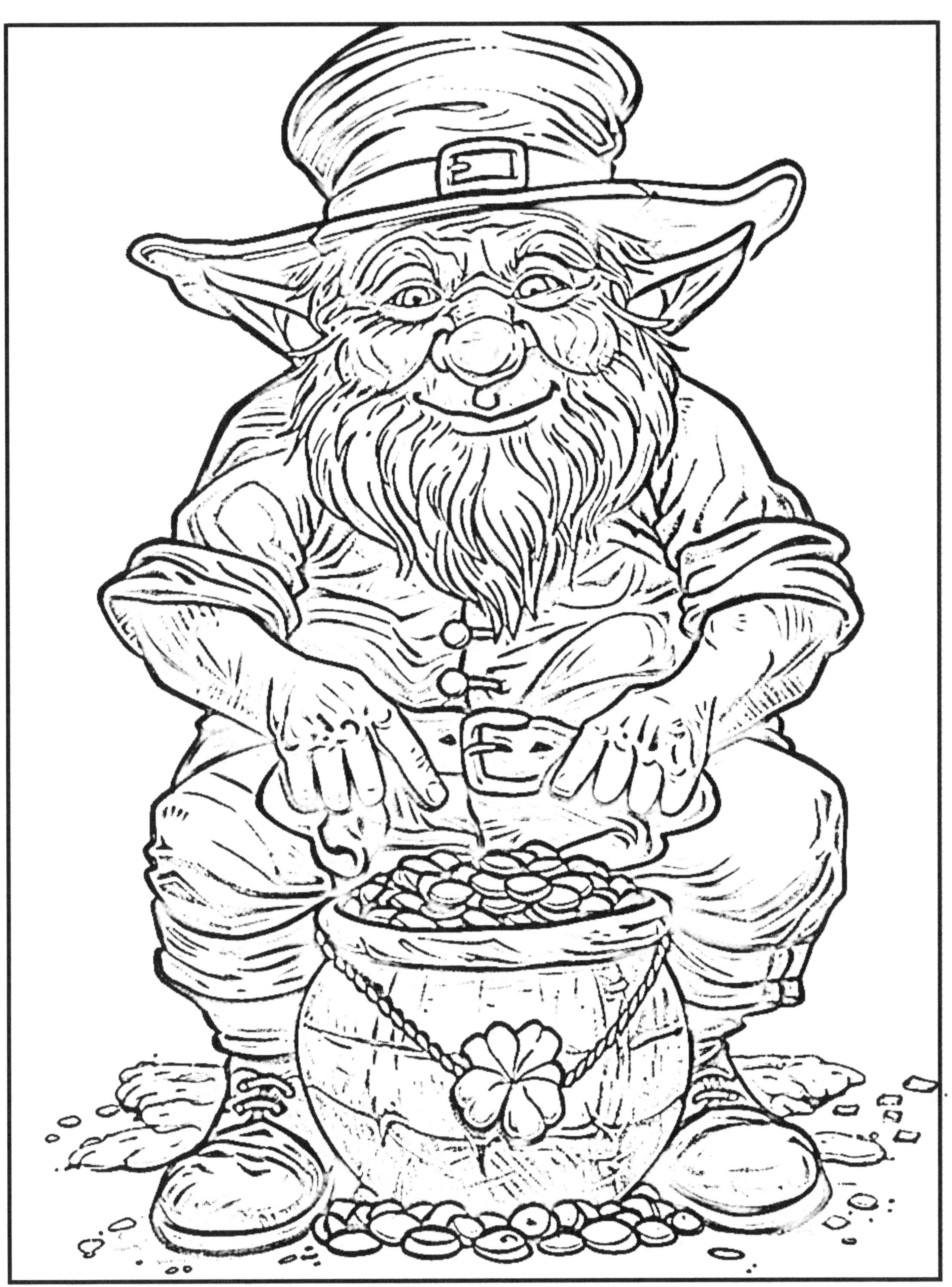

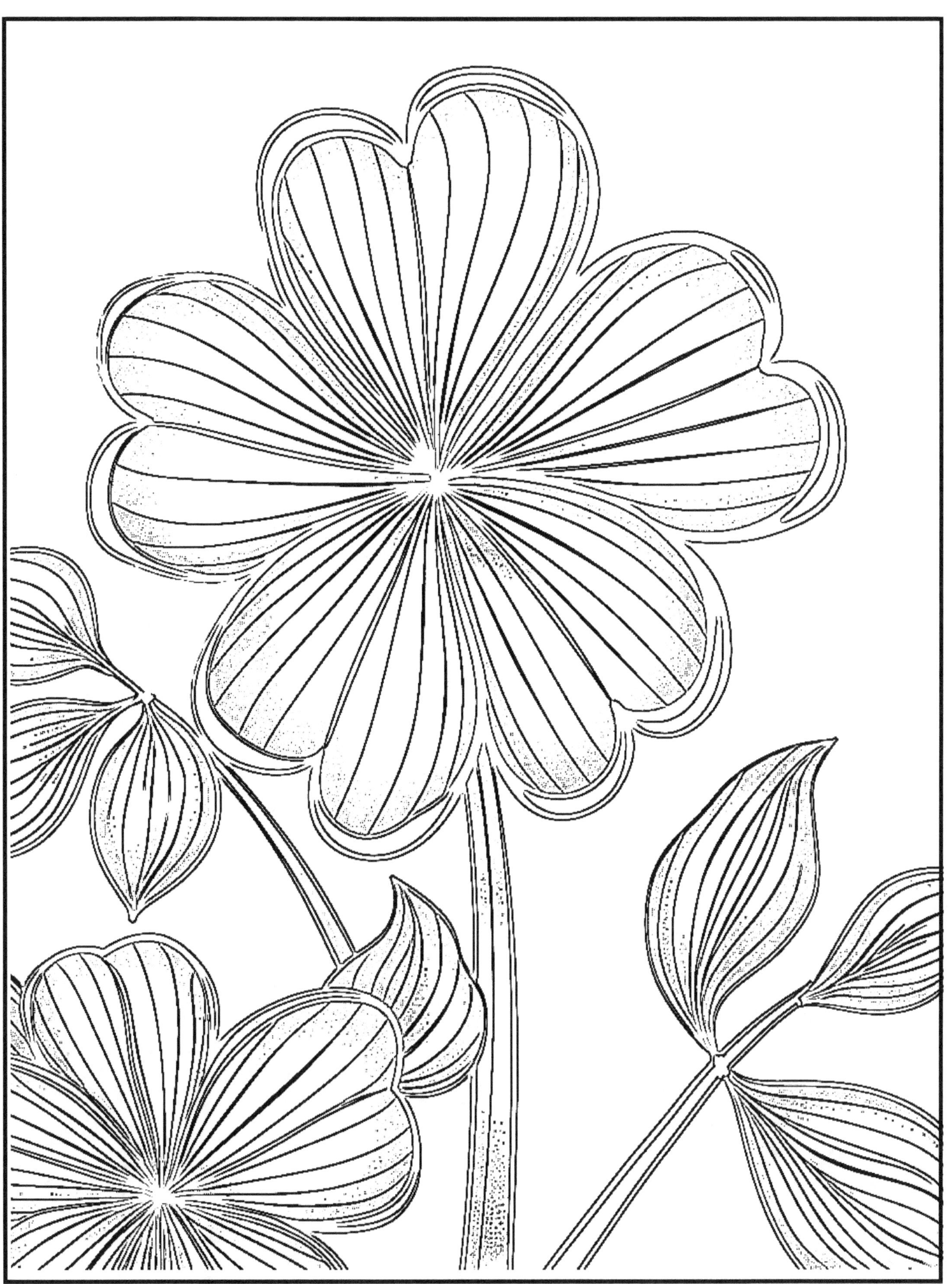

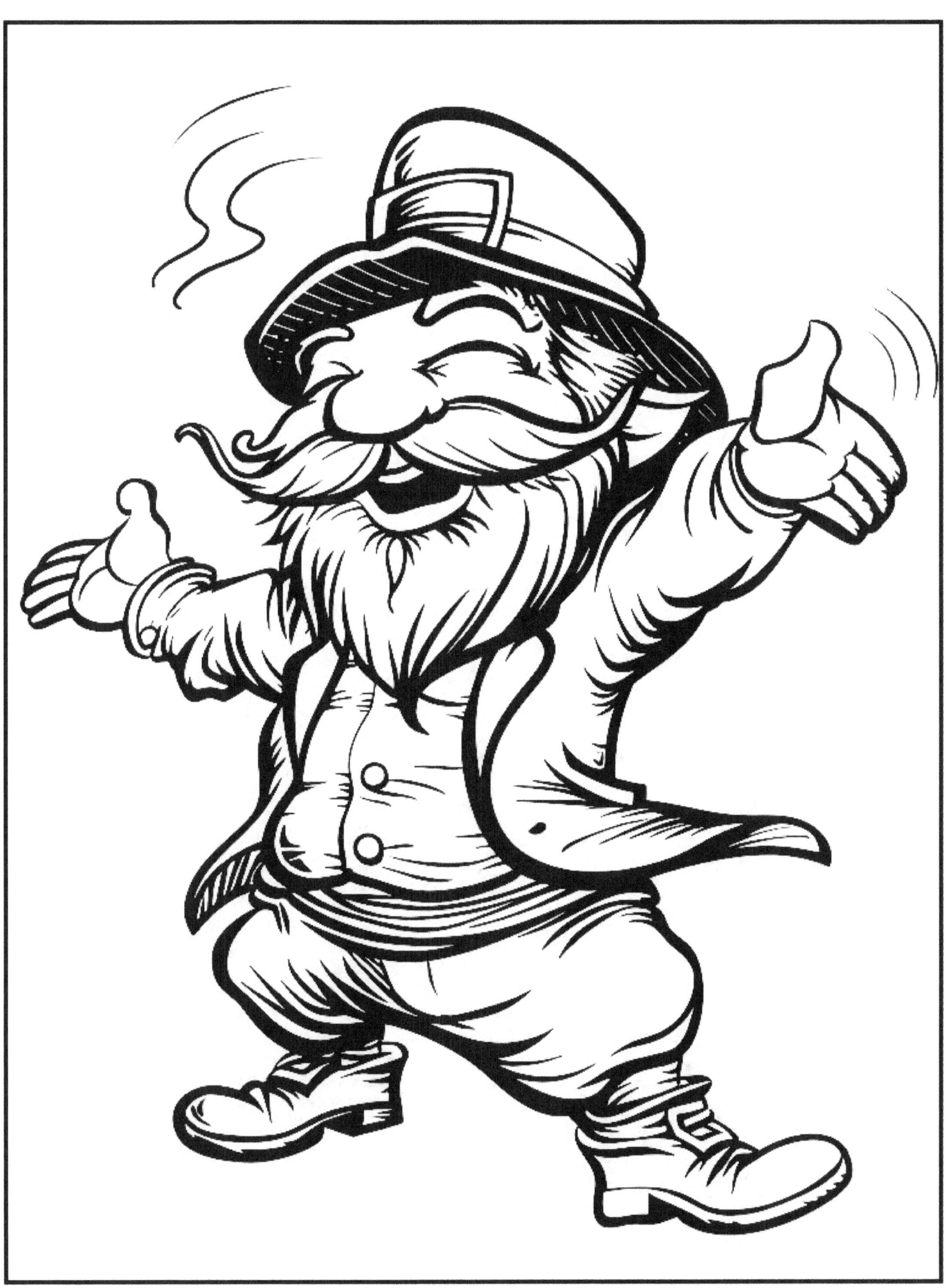

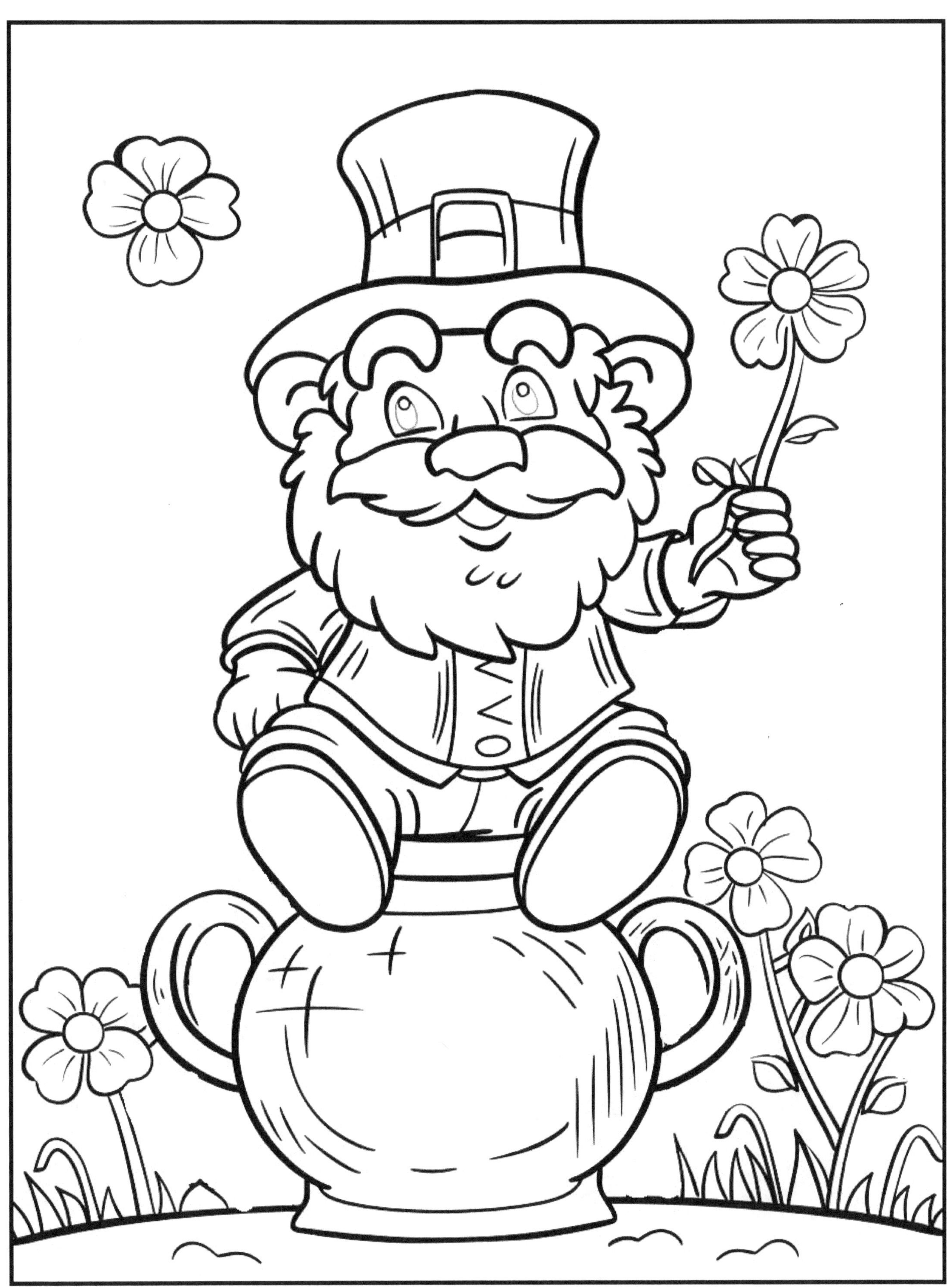

Thank you for your purchase!
Your feedback is greatly appreciated!

It's through your feedback, support and reviews that we're able to create the best books possible and serve more people.

We would be extremely grateful if you could take just 60 seconds to kindly leave an honest review of the book on Amazon. Please share your feedback and thoughts for others to see.

To do so, simply find the book on Amazon's website (or wherever you purchased the book from) and locate the section to leave a review. Select a star rating and write a couple of sentences.

That's it! Thank you so much for your support.

Review this product

Share your thoughts with other customers

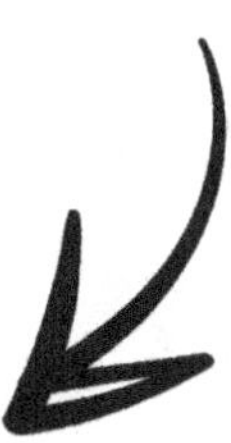